THE AUTHOR

Stephen Pile is a Renaiss...
unable to do a vast rang...

The Not Terribly Good Club of Great Britain

Western civilization is obsessed with success, even though most of us have a genuine flair for the exact opposite. Three years ago Stephen Pile decided to do something about it: he formed the Not Terribly Good Club of Great Britain. To get into the Club you had to be not terribly good at something and preferably downright awful. Members addressed the Club on the things they did worst or couldn't do at all. Sometimes they would give displays and win standing ovations. Over the years they held appalling musical evenings, art exhibitions and so on until the membership grew from 20 to 200. The book contains an application form for membership.

THE BOOK OF HEROIC FAILURES

THE OFFICIAL HANDBOOK OF THE NOT TERRIBLY GOOD CLUB OF GREAT BRITAIN

BY STEPHEN PILE

WITH CARTOONS BY BILL TIDY

FUTURA PUBLICATIONS
LONDON

A Futura Book

First published in Great Britain by
Routledge & Kegan Paul Ltd in 1979

FIRST FUTURA PUBLICATIONS EDITION 1980

ISBN 0 7088 1908 7

Photoset by
Rowland Phototypesetting Limited,
Bury St Edmunds, Suffolk

Printed in Great Britain by
Hazell, Watson & Viney Ltd
Aylesbury.

Futura Publications Limited
110 Warner Road, Camberwell
London SE5

DEDICATION

To all those who have written terrible books on how to be a success, I dedicate this terrible book on how it's perfectly all right to be incompetent for hours on end, because I am and so is everyone I know.

CONTENTS

ACKNOWLEDGMENTS
p. 9

INTRODUCTION
p. 11

ONE
THE WORLD OF WORK
p. 15

TWO
OFF DUTY
p. 43

THREE
LAW AND ORDER
p. 77

FOUR
PLAYING THE GAME
p. 97

FIVE
THE CULTURAL SIDE OF THINGS
p. 113

CONTENTS

SIX
THE GLORY OF THE STAGE
p. 139

SEVEN
WAR AND PEACE
p. 157

EIGHT
THE BUSINESS OF POLITICS
p. 175

NINE
LOVE AND MARRIAGE
p. 189

TEN
STORIES WE FAILED TO PIN DOWN
p. 201

ELEVEN
THE ART OF BEING WRONG
p. 211

ACKNOWLEDGMENTS

I should like to thank all who have cheerfully suggested
themselves as the worst in a given sphere;

All who have cheerfully suggested other people;

Miss Peta Stuart-Hunt for organizing my otherwise
chaotic research;

Bill Addis for taking away my filing system when I could
no longer work it and for general support;

William Fowler and Antony Preston for help on military
matters;

Roy Plomley for permission to retell his *Desert Island
Discs* disaster;

Leslie Halliwell and Paladin Books for permission to
quote from *The Filmgoers Companion*;

The *New Statesman* for permission to quote from their
article on the least successful handcuffing;

The Guinness Book of Records for permission to quote a
fact or two;

Mandy Orlebar and Dad for typing;

Barclay, Fiona, Stephen and Mum for food at all the
appropriate moments.

INTRODUCTION

If a thing's worth doing, it is worth doing badly.
G. K. CHESTERTON

Success is overrated.

Everyone craves it despite daily proof that man's real genius lies in quite the opposite direction. Incompetence is what we are good at: it is the quality that marks us off from animals and we should learn to revere it.

Of course, the occasional Segovia does slip through the net with the result that we all cut sandwiches and queue in the rain for hours to watch him play the guitar without once dropping his plectrum down the hole. But this book is not for the likes of him. It is for us: we, the less than good, who spend hours shaking the plectrum out and impress only our mothers.

Here, collected in one anthology for the first time, are the great names: Coates, Falconer, the abysmal Nuttall, the immortal Carolino, the dire Foster-Jenkins and McGonagall. People who were so bad in their chosen sphere of endeavour that their names live on as a beacon for future generations.

THE NOT TERRIBLY GOOD CLUB OF GREAT BRITAIN

I am sure that I am not the only one who cannot do things and the slightest investigation reveals that no one else can do anything either. This being the case, it seems to me that Mankind spends a disproportionate amount of time talking about the things he does well, when these few blades of grass are surrounded by vast prairies of inadequacy which are much more interesting.

So, in 1976 the Not Terribly Good Club of Great Britain was formed with myself, cocooned in administrative chaos, as president.

To qualify for membership you just had to be not terribly good at something (fishing, small talk, batik, anything) and then attend meetings at which people talked about and gave public demonstrations of the things they could not do. We had some glorious evenings when you heard snatches of heartwarming conversation ('Yes, sheep are difficult' – Not Terribly Good Artist).

In September 1976, twenty members hand-picked from all fields of incompetence gathered for the inaugural dinner at an exquisitely inferior London restaurant. We had mushroom soup (which is now filling one member's cavity wall in Kew) and the other courses would have been more or less edible had they not been delayed in the oven for over an hour by our dull and seemingly interminable speeches.

These were of a gratifyingly low standard. Our Not Terribly Good Parachutist, an extremely petite girl, outlined some of the problems caused by being so light that when she jumps in breezy conditions she invariably goes up. By the time she lands the pilot has usually finished his tea and gone home. My own presidential address was so dull it got a standing ovation, but I was later thrown out as president for stopping a soup tureen from falling over.

So inauspicious was the inaugural dinner that, three months later, we held a musical evening at which we all played our instruments until we were too overcome to continue. It finally ground to a halt when one member sang a protest song exposing a series of injustices, all of which had been eradicated over a century ago: cockfighting, child chimney sweeps, and so on.

Then came the art exhibition, 'Salon des Incompetents'. Held in a Territorial Army drill hall in the summer of 1977, the membership launched 'incompetisme' upon a completely indifferent world. Our Press Officer sent out only one release to a magazine specializing in bird-cages. Showing a total lack of interest quite admirable in journalists, they threw it away.

It was an exhibition of uniquely impoverished art work that included a *Shelf Portrait* which was not a misprint in the catalogue as everyone assumed.

Among other works were *The Death of St Sebastian* which featured a skeleton with a darts board behind it, and my own *Edible Last Supper* which had real food glued to it. (I always get peckish looking at other artists' *Last Suppers*. With mine, the onlooker may tuck in with them and help himself to St Matthew's cheese and pineapple rolls, or to one of Doubting Thomas's chocolate cupcakes.)

In fact, we first approached the Tate Gallery to see if we could hold our exhibition there. We got a polite letter by return of post from an Assistant in the Modern Collection.

'Thank you for your inquiry', it said. 'While we would like to help your artistic endeavours, we feel that we could not allow you to knock down the portico and three interior walls of the Tate, as you suggest, in order to get your larger exhibits into the building. This might cause serious problems with the Permanent Collection.

'As for your inquiry about daubing a work of your own on top of an existing mural, you will have to take this up with out Conservation Department. I am afraid that this would apply even to "one of the older ones". I hope your exhibition goes well.'

Our most recent event was a New Year's Eve party held in mid-December. It was the only date that suited all the members. An erratic jazz band that defied dancing took us towards midnight and a guest speaker gave an illustrated talk on his disastrous holiday in Greenland. Unfortunately, his slides did not fit the projector and so they had to be passed around the audience of eighty by hand.

Other events included a First Aid display by a team of enthusiastic short nurses who demonstrated how they would bandage the head of an unusually tall invalid. (They climbed up him.)

Plans are now well advanced for our summer rowing regatta. However, at present we have only one air bed and, unless a second vessel is forthcoming, the races will be more monotonous than is strictly necessary.

Many Club members have been active in helping me to collect information for this handbook. The definitive 'worst ever' was hard to come by in our success-crazed society. People do not widely realize that to be really bad at something requires skill, dedication and intense orginality of vision.

The following entries are the worst that we have come across. If you are even worse, then I would be fascinated to hear from you.

HOW TO READ THIS BOOK

I have divided this history up into manageable chunks of information. The best thing is to use it like a swimming pool – dip in occasionally, but come out quickly and lie somewhere, exhausted, with a strong drink.

Before we set off on our conducted tour around some pretty inspired fallibility, awarding wooden spoons wreathed in laurel, it only remains to echo the words of Philaster Chase Johnson while encouraging readers to plough through his magazine article in 1920.

'Cheer up, the worst is yet to come.'

ONE

THE WORLD OF WORK

Our business in life is not to succeed,
but to continue to fail in good spirits.
Robert Louis Stevenson

THE WORST BUS SERVICE
THE LEAST SUCCESSFUL SAVING
THE WORST BROADCAST
THE LEAST SUCCESSFUL NEWSPAPER
THE WORST COMPUTER
THE WORST SHIP
THE LEAST SUCCESSFUL SAFETY FILM
THE LEAST SUCCESSFUL ANIMAL RESCUE
THE WORST CANAL CLEARANCE
THE WORST CANAL

Success: the one unpardonable sin
against one's fellow man.
Ambrose Bierce

THE LEAST SUCCESSFUL EXPLORER

Thomas Nuttall (1786–1859) was a pioneer botanist whose main field of study was the flora of remote parts of North-west America. As an explorer, however his work was characterized by the fact that he was almost permanently lost. During his expedition of 1812 his colleagues frequently had to light beacons in the evening to help him find his way back to camp.

One night he completely failed to return and a search party was sent out. As it approached him in the darkness Nuttall assumed they were Indians and tried to escape. The annoyed rescuers pursued him for three days through bush and river until he accidently wandered back into the camp. On another occasion Nuttall was lost again and lay down exhausted. He looked so pathetic that a passing Indian, instead of scalping him, picked him up, carried him three miles to the river and paddled him home in a canoe.

THE LEAST SUCCESSFUL CIRCUS ACT

When the circus came to New York in 1978, the publicity posters carried the question: 'Can aerialist Tito Gaona – spinning at 75 miles an hour – accomplish the most difficult acrobatic feat of the twentieth century?' The short answer to this was 'No'.

Every night for nine months Tito attempted the first ever quadruple somersault in mid-air from a flying trapeze 60 feet above the ground. Every night for nine months he got part way through, missed his catcher and plunged into the safety net. At Madison Square Gardens he sustained a whole season of magnificent failure. Asked if he had ever done it, Tito replied: 'Yes, once. At rehearsals and only my family were watching'.

THE LEAST SUCCESSFUL CONTORTION ACT

As part of his act while appearing in Roberts Brothers Circus at Southend in August 1978, Janos the Incredible Rubber Man was lowered to the floor hanging from a trapeze, with his legs wrapped somewhere behind his head. Normally, he rolls around for a spell to the applause of amazed audiences, before reverting to a more conventional human posture.

On this occasion he just sat there. 'I couldn't move,' he said later, by way of explanation.

The situation was resolved by a circus official, Mr Kenneth Julian. 'We put Janos in the back of my van and took him to hospital.' Doctors wrestled with the problem for thirty minutes and ordered the Incredible Rubber Man to lie flat for a week.

THE WORST MAGICIAN

It is quite possible that if Tommy Cooper's tricks had worked, no one would have heard of him. Happily, however, his magic was, from the start, blessed with an almost operatic badness. He has become a much loved household name.

It may be of interest to hear how this great man discovered his unique gifts. At the age of 17, while an apprentice shipwright, he appeared in a public concert held in the firm's canteen at Hyde in Essex. Intending to give a serious display of magic, he walked on to the stage. As soon as the curtains parted, he forgot all his lines.

For a while he just stood there, opening his mouth only to close it again. The audience was spellbound. 'All right', he thought, 'get on with it'.

He got on with it and everything went wrong. His grand finale was the milk bottle trick. 'You have a bottle full of milk', he told the entranced audience, 'and you put paper over the top. You turn the bottle upside down, and take the paper away. The milk stays in.'

With bated breath, the audience watched. He turned the bottle. He paused for effect. He took away the paper. Drenched. All over him.

As if he had not done enough already, Mr Cooper then got stage fright and began working his mouth furiously without any sound coming out. At this point he started to tremble and walked off, perspiring heavily. Once in the wings, he heard the massed cheers of a standing ovation. His future glory was assured.

THE BRITISH RAIL CHAIRMAN
WHO CAUGHT THE WRONG TRAIN

In July 1978 Sir Peter Parker, the Chairman of British Rail, set off to attend a meeting with Cumbria County Council.

Delayed by traffic, Sir Peter arrived at Crewe Station just as his train was leaving. He tore through the ticket barrier, waved a B.R. pass, and leaped on.

As the journey progressed, it dawned on him that, far from being on the express for Carlisle, he was aboard the non-stopper for London.

Eventually he persuaded the guard to throw a note wrapped round a coin out of the window as the train thundered through Tamworth Station in Staffordshire. It said, 'Please apologize to Cumbria Council and tell them I won't be able to make it.' As soon as he got back to London, he set off for the North once more. This time by 'plane.

'It just goes to show that it can happen to anyone,' he said.

THE WORST BUS SERVICE

Can any bus service rival the fine Hanley to Bagnall route in Staffordshire? In 1976 it was reported that the buses no longer stopped for passengers.

This came to light when one of them, Mr Bill Hancock, complained that buses on the outward journey regularly sailed past queues of up to thirty people.

Councillor Arthur Cholerton then made transport history by stating that if these buses stopped to pick up passengers they would disrupt the time-table.

THE WORST LOCOMOTIVE DESIGNER

Few engineers can equal the achievement of Francis Webb, a locomotive designer for the London and North

Western Railway at the end of the last century. In one book on locomotive design the index reads: 'Webb, Francis – his incompetence'.

Many of his early engines were quite outstanding – they were no faster or more powerful than other designs and yet were more expensive, less efficient and much worse at starting. Despite this, he improved on them in such a way that they would frequently not start at all. His Teutonic class of locomotives, for example, had two pairs of driving wheels which were not connected and were capable of turning simultaneously in opposite directions. The engine would remain motionless, puffing violently, with the two pairs of wheels spinning to no effect. To overcome this problem, the LNWR frequently had to use two engines, one of Webb's and the other of a different design, simply to get the train started.

THE LEAST SUCCESSFUL OPERATION

After the birth of their second child, Mr and Mrs Len Trott decided that their family was large enough. So in March 1978 she went into hospital for a hysterectomy. Eighteen months later she gave birth to a 6lb 5½oz son called Martin.

THE LEAST SUCCESSFUL SAVING

In 1974 Bramber Parish Council decided to go without street lighting for three days as a saving. Afterwards the parish treasurer was pleased to announce that, as a result, electricity to the value of £11.59 had been saved. He added, however, that there was an £18.48 bill for switching the electricity off and another of £12.00 for switching it on again. It had cost the council £18.89 to spend three days in darkness.

THE BIGGEST BANKRUPTCY

British bankruptcy history was made in 1978 by Mr William Stern. The 43-year-old property dealer's assets totalled £10,070. His total liabilities were in excess of £100,000,000.

Hearing the case in the London Bankruptcy Court, Mr Alan Sales, the Official Receiver, said, 'This bankruptcy has been described as the world's biggest, but really it is a very ordinary bankruptcy with noughts at the end.'

THE MOST UNSUCCESSFUL ATTEMPT TO WORK THROUGH A LUNCH HOUR

Mr Stanley Hird surely set a record in June 1978 when trying to catch up on some paperwork. At one o'clock his carpet factory outside Bradford was deserted and he settled down for an uninterrupted hour. At ten past one a cow fell through the roof. The cow had clambered on to the roof from the adjoining field. For thirty seconds they stared at each other and then the cow, who had also been planning a quiet lunch hour, lowered her head and charged. This continued for some minutes, during which time Mr Hird retreated steadily towards the door as the cow scattered stacks of wool. Eventually the heifer, whose name was Rosie, stopped to chew a green carpet and Mr Hird escaped into the corridor. Here he met a farmer who inquired if he had seen a heifer. Police, firemen and an elaborate set of pulleys were needed to extract the animal.

THE LEAST SUCCESSFUL WEATHER REPORT

After severe flooding in Jeddah in January 1979, the Arab News gave the following bulletin:

'We regret we are unable to give you the weather. We rely on weather reports from the airport, which is closed because of the weather. Whether we are able to give you the weather tomorrow depends on the weather.'

THE WORST BROADCAST

Few broadcasters have given more unalloyed pleasure than Lieutenant Commander Tommy Woodroofe. He leaped to public prominence with his now famous commentary on the illumination of the fleet at Spithead in 1937.

Before the broadcast the Commander had joined in celebrations with slightly too much enthusiasm. The result was an exquisitely incoherent talk punctuated by pauses of anything up to eleven seconds.

'At the present moment', he began, 'the whole fleet is lit up. When I say "lit up" I mean lit up by fairy lamps. It's fantastic. It isn't a fleet at all. It's just . . . It's fairyland. The whole fleet is in fairyland. Now if you'll follow me through . . . if you don't mind . . . the next few moments you'll find the fleet doing odd things.'

There then followed a lengthy pause. 'I'm sorry I was telling some people to shut up talking', the commander explained delightfully.

At this point all lights on the fleet were turned out so that rockets could be fired. The commander's reaction was: 'It's gone. It's gone. There's no fleet. It's . . . It's disappeared. No magician who ever could have waved his wand could have waved it with more acumen than he has now at the present moment. The fleet's gone. It's disappeared.

'I was talking to you in the middle of this damn . . . (coughs) in the middle of this fleet and what's happened is the fleet's gone and disappeared and gone.'

At this point Woodroofe was faded out; an announcer said: 'That is the end of the Spithead commentary' and dance music came on.

Commander Woodroofe said afterwards that he had been 'overcome by emotion'.

THE MOST UNSUCCESSFUL TV COMMERCIAL

The comedienne Pat Coombs is the proud holder of the record for the largest number of unsuccessful 'takes' for a television commercial. In 1973, while making a breakfast cereal advertisement, she forgot her lines twenty-eight times. On each occasion she forgot the same thing –

the name of the product. When asked five years later what the product was, she replied: 'I still can't remember. It was some sort of muesli, but the name was practically unpronounceable. They were very kind to me, but that only made it worse. I had total stage-fright every time the camera came near me. With each take I got worse. It's put me off cereal for life.'

The commercial was never finished and the product was taken off the market soon afterwards.

THE LEAST SUCCESSFUL NEWSPAPER

Described on billboards as 'Britain's most fearless newspaper', the *Commonwealth Sentinel* opened on 6th February, 1965 and closed on the 7th. Designed to cater for all Commonwealth citizens, the paper was founded by Mr Lionel Burleigh in London. He spent a hectic week collecting the advertisements, writing the stories and seeing the first issue through the press. Then Mr Burleigh received a phone call from the police.

'Are you anything to do with the *Commonwealth Sentinel*?' asked a constable, encouraged by an hysterical hotel porter. 'Because there are 50,000 of them outside the entrance to Brown's Hotel and they're blocking Albemarle Street.'

'We had forgotten to arrange any distribution,' Mr Burleigh said later, 'and they were just dumped outside the hotel where I was staying. To my knowledge we only sold one copy. I still have the shilling in my drawer'. It was sold by Mr Burleigh's daughter to a passer-by. This caused so much excitement that a photograph was taken of the transaction.

THE LEAST SUCCESSFUL
NEWS HOUND

V. S. Pritchett is a celebrated literary critic, but we can overlook this in view of his contribution to hard news reporting.

In the 1920s he took a job as a reporter on the *Christian Science Monitor*.

Long after the event he said about his time as the *Monitor*'s correspondent in Northern Ireland: 'I simply didn't know what news was. I missed every important occasion. Even now I don't know what news is.'

He once missed the resignation of a Cabinet Minister because he 'couldn't see how it mattered'. His finest achievement came in 1922 when he was sent to cover the war in Spanish Morocco. 'Any enterprising reporter would have gone into the hills to interview the Moroccan leader Abdul Krin, but not me. The idea filled me with horror and I vigorously abstained. All I heard was a lot of gunfire in the evenings', he said, 'but it was a lovely country.'

THE LEAST ACCURATE
NEWSPAPER REPORT

Newspaper reporters make mistakes, of course, but few have been more innovative than the one who contributed a personality profile of a local man called 'Harris' to the *Wiltshire Times and Chippenham News* in 1963. The following week the paper carried a magnificent apology.

Mr Harris, it said, has asked us to point out a number of inaccuracies in our story. After returning from India, he served in Ireland for four years and not six months as stated; he never farmed at Heddington, particularly not at Coate Road Farm as stated; he has never counted cycling or walking among his hobbies; he is not a member of 54 hunts; and he did not have an eye removed at Chippenham Hospital after an air raid on Calne.

'My only disappointment when interviewing him', wrote the reporter in his original article, 'was that I could not spare more time with this raconteur.'

THE FULLEST ERRATA LIST

A booklet entitled *The History of Cornish Pubs* gained extreme popularity in 1978 on account of its impressive errata list.

It contained 140 corrections to a 70-page survey. High spots include:

Page 3 line 1	for 'assuming' read 'unassuming'
Page 8 line 54	for 'White Hart' read 'White Horse'
Page 13 line 49	for 'major' read 'minor'
Page 32 line 19	for 'Mews' read 'mess'
Page 33 line 44	for 'Bishop and Wool' read 'Bridge on Wool'
Page 63 line 6	for 'Queen's Arms' read 'Queen's Head'
Page 73	Moulded ceilings line 5 delete ship, Fowey line 6 for Batallick read Botallack. Pannelling line 2 for Bosliwick read Boslowick.

In the book, sub-titled 'pubs with a storey to tell', the engagingly modest editor says, 'We must apologize for the minor mistakes which have cropped up between correcting the proof and printing. Some are my fault, others, like a car one takes in to have repaired, the fault is repaired, but others occur! A few we have not corrected, especially punctuations! It should be possible to insert these in the text.'

THE MOST MISPRINTS IN A NEWSPAPER

This record is claimed for a page in *The Times* of London on 15 March 1978; it contains 78 misprints.

One story starts 'Sir Harold Wilson's action in making public a oss' and goes on to deal with a braodcast involving the governm and comparahle pay claims.

These errors were caused by an industrial dispute and do not, in any case, have the sheer style of the *Guardian* which can do this sort of thing quite unaided. Among its most famous misprints was a review of the opera *Doris Gudenov*.

THE GREATEST MATHEMATICAL ERROR

The Mariner I space probe was launched from Cape Canaveral on 28 July 1962 towards Venus. After 13 minutes' flight a booster engine would give acceleration up to 25,820 mph; after 44 minutes 9,800 solar cells would unfold; after 80 days a computer would calculate the final course corrections and after 100 days the craft would circle the unknown planet, scanning the mysterious cloud in which is it bathed.

However, with an efficiency that is truly heartening, Mariner I plunged into the Atlantic Ocean only four minutes after take off.

Inquiries later revealed that a minus sign had been omitted from the instructions fed into the computer. 'It was human error', a launch spokesman said.

This minus sign cost £4,280,000.

THE MOST POINTLESS RADIO INTERVIEW

One of Britain's most popular radio programmes is 'Desert Island Discs' in which a celebrity is asked to imagine that, for unspecified reasons, he is trapped on a desert island with his eight favourite records.

In the early 1970s the programme's presenter, Roy Plomley was keen to get the novelist Alistair Maclean on to his programme. As a writer of adventure stories, it was felt he might fit the role of a castaway and give a gripping broadcast.

This was soon arranged, despite Maclean's known reluctance to give interviews.

Mr Plomley arranged to meet him for lunch at the Savile Club in London. They got on extremely well.

During lunch Mr Plomley asked, 'Which part of the year do you put aside for your writing?'

'Writing?' said Maclean.

'Yes – your books – *Guns of Navarone*.'

'I'm not Alistair Maclean, the writer.'

'No?'

'No. I'm in charge of the Ontario Tourist Bureau.'

With no alternative, the two set off for the studio. During the recording an increasingly agitated producer urged: 'Ask him about his books.' 'He hasn't written any,' replied the broadcaster.

The programme was never broadcast.

THE MOST INACCURATE VALUE OF PI (π)

Pi (π) is a mathematical constant which is the ratio of the circumference of the circle to its diameter. It is a never-ending number and, for most calculations, is taken to its third decimal place (3.142).

However, in 1897 the General Assembly of Indiana passed a Bill ruling that the value of Pi was four. This ensured that all mathematical and engineering calculations in the State would be wrong. It would, for example, mean that a pendulum clock would gain about fifteen minutes every hour.

THE WORST COMPUTER

It is widely suggested that computers improve efficiency. Lovers of vintage chaos might remember the computer installed in 1975 by Avon County Council to pay staff wages.

The computer's spree started off in a small way, paying a school caretaker £75 an hour instead of 75 pence. Then it got ambitious and did not pay a canteen worker at all for seven weeks.

Before long it got positively confident and paid a janitor £2,600 for a week's work. He sent the cheque back and received another for the same amount by return of post.

There was now no stopping it. A deputy headmistress received her year's annual salary once a month; heads of department earned less than their assistants, and some people had more tax deducted in a week than they earned all year.

In February 1975 two hundred and eighty employees on the Council payroll attended a protest meeting. Of these, only eight had been paid the correct salary. They all went on strike.

THE LEAST SUCCESSFUL FIRE ENGINE

In 1973 a fire broke out at 2 Crisp Road, Henley. The occupants telephoned the local fire brigade only to find that it was taking part in 'Operation Greenfly', a simulated exercise to douse an imaginary fire on the village green.

The alarmed occupants next telephoned nearby Wallington Fire Station who said they would send a fire engine immediately. Half way down Bix Hill, the cab burst into flames and the firemen struggled out, choking.

Although there were 400 gallons of water on board, this could not be used, since the suction pump was operated from the cab which was now full of smoke.

At this point the local fire brigade, on its way back from Operation Greenfly, drove past. They pulled to a halt and said they had very little water left, having just waterlogged the village green.

They did what they could, while the Wallington firemen sheepishly asked passing motorists if they had any fire extinguishers.

The fire at 2 Crisp Road was put out by energetic locals throwing water.

THE WORST SHIP

Between 1953, when it was built, and 1976, when it sank, the *Argo Merchant* suffered every known form of maritime disaster.

In 1967 the ship took eight months to sail from Japan to America. It collided with a Japanese ship, caught fire three times and had to stop for repairs five times.

In 1968 there was a mutiny and in 1969 she went aground off Borneo for thirty-four hours. In the next five years she was laid up in Curaçao, grounded off Sicily and towed to New York.

In 1976 her boilers broke down six times and she once had to travel with two red lights displayed, indicating that the crew could no longer control the ship's movements because steering and engine had failed. She was banned from Philadelphia, Boston and the Panama Canal.

To round off a perfect year she ran aground and sank off Cape Cod depositing the country's largest oil slick on the doorstep of Massachussetts.

At the time of the final grounding the ship had been 'lost' for fifteen hours. The crew was eighteen miles off course and navigating by the stars, because modern equipment had broken down. What is more, the West Indian helmsman could not read the Greek handwriting showing the course to be steered.

A naval expert afterwards described the ship as 'a disaster looking for somewhere to happen'.

THE LEAST SUCCESSFUL SAFETY FILM

In 1976 the British Aircraft Corporation showed a film on the dangers of not wearing protective goggles to employees at its Preston factory. It was so horrific that thirteen employees had to be helped out by workmates and State Registered Nurses.

One scene was so realistic that a welder fell off his chair in fright and had to have seven stitches. During the same scene another worker fainted and had to be carried out. In one full-colour close-up a group of machine minders had to be led out feeling sick and faint.

The divisional safety officer, Mr Ron Hesketh, said the film was being withdrawn because it was not safe. 'We are very keen to get over the point of eye protection,' he said, 'but at this point in time we have decided not to take any chances. We seem to have had at least one person keeling over on every course during the safety campaign.'

ODEON

SON OF FRANKENSTEIN MEETS DRACULAS WOLFMAN

SEATS IN ALL PARTS

'STUFF THIS FOR A LARK I'M OFF TO B.A.C!'

THE LEAST SUCCESSFUL
SECURITY OPERATION

Worried that ground staff were stealing miniature bottles of whisky from a Pan-Am aircraft, security guards set a trap.

In the summer of 1978 they wired up a cuckoo clock inside the drinks cabinet so arranged that it would stop whenever the door was opened. This, they said, would reveal the exact time of the theft.

They omitted, however, to tell the plane's crew with the result that a stewardess, Miss Susan Becker, assumed it was a bomb.

She alerted the pilot of the Boeing 727 who made an emergency landing at Berlin where eighty passengers left in a hurry through fire exits.

A Pan-Am spokesman said afterwards that the miniature bottles of whisky on the plane cost 17 pence each. The cost of the emergency landing was £6,500.

THE LEAST SUCCESSFUL
ANIMAL RESCUE

The firemen's strike of 1978 made possible one of the great animal rescue attempts of all time. Valiantly, the British Army had taken over emergency firefighting and on 14 January they were called out by an elderly lady in South London to retrieve her cat which had become trapped up a tree. They arrived with impressive haste and soon discharged their duty. So grateful was the lady that she invited them all in for tea. Driving off later, with fond farewells completed, they ran over the cat and killed it.

THE VET WHO SURPRISED A COW

In the course of his duties in August 1977, a Dutch veterinary surgeon was required to treat an ailing cow. To investigate its internal gases he inserted a tube into that end of the animal not capable of facial expression and struck a match. The jet of flame set fire first to some bales of hay and then to the whole farm causing damage estimated at £45,000. The vet was later fined £140 for starting a fire in a manner surprising to the magistrates. The cow escaped with shock.

THE MAN WHO ALMOST INVENTED THE VACUUM CLEANER

The man officially credited with inventing the vacuum cleaner is Hubert Cecil Booth. However, he got the idea from a man who almost invented it.

In 1901 Booth visited a London music-hall. On the bill was an American inventor with his wonder machine for removing dust from carpets.

The machine comprised a box about one foot square with a bag on top. After watching the act – which made everyone in the front six rows sneeze – Booth went round to the inventor's dressing room.

'It should suck not blow,' said Booth, coming straight to the point. 'Suck?', exclaimed the enraged inventor. 'Your machine just moves the dust around the room,' Booth informed him. 'Suck? Suck? Sucking is not possible,' was the inventor's reply and he stormed out. Booth proved that it was by the simple expedient of kneeling down, pursing his lips and sucking the back of an armchair. 'I almost choked' he said afterwards.

THE LEAST CONVENIENT POST BOX

In March 1979 workmen at Ballymacra, County Antrim, replaced a telegraph pole upon which a pillar box was fixed.

The workmen did not have the official keys needed to release the clips that fastened the box to the pole. So they raised it over the top of the old one and then slipped it down the new one. The new pole turned out to be thicker than the old one and the post box came to rest nine feet above the ground.

It remained in this position for three weeks during which time some post still managed to get through. 'I am told', said Mr Ernie McDermott, the postmaster, 'that someone provided a step ladder. The mind boggles.'

THE LEAST SUCCESSFUL EXIT

The residents of Bennett Court, an Old Folks Home in Otley, Yorkshire had long wanted a fence around their home to give it more privacy. Early in 1979 the Leeds Council workers arrived in their lorry with picks, shovels and planks of wood. They took five days to erect the 3½ feet high and 100 yard long fence. After they had completed it they noticed that they had not left a gap to drive their lorry out.

'It was like watching a Laurel and Hardy film,' said Mrs Elizabeth Ann Whittaker, who saw the whole creative process. 'You could see them looking at the fence, then at the lorry, then at the fence again. Some of us had wondered about the lorry, but we didn't want to interfere.'

A council spokesman said: 'It was an oversight. Maybe they got carried away in their work.' The workers returned next morning to knock down part of the fence and recover their lorry.

THE WORST CANAL CLEARANCE

In 1978 workers were sent to dredge a murky stretch of the Chesterfield–Stockwith canal. Their task was to remove all the rubbish and leave the canal clear. They were soon disturbed during their teabreak by a policeman who said he was investigating a giant whirlpool in the canal. When they got back, however, the whirlpool had gone and so had a one and a half mile stretch of the canal. In its place was a seamless stretch of mud thickly punctuated with old prams, bedsteads and rusting bicycle accessories. In addition to this the workmen found a flotilla of irate holidaymakers stranded on their boats in a browr. sludge.

Among the first pieces of junk they hauled out had been the 200-year-old plug that alone ensured the canal's continuing existence. 'We didn't know there was a plug', said one workman explaining that all the records had been lost in a fire during the war. 'Anything can happen on a canal', a spokesman for the British Waterways Board said afterwards.

THE WORST CANAL

In 1840 a construction company was asked to build a waterway between two lakes in Western Ireland, Corrib and Mask. With an inspiration not given to everyone, they built it entirely on porous limestone. The result was that no sooner had water been poured in than it drained away. In an effort to correct this fault, a clay bed was laid. However, it was soon found that one of the lakes was several feet lower than the other. As the work neared completion the workmen realised that they were asking water to run uphill. At this point the project was abandoned, leaving a quay that has never seen a boat and a bridge under which nothing has ever flowed. [Lest you should think this another Irish joke ascribing all incompetence to the Emerald Isle, it should be said that the canal's designer was an Englishman.]

THE LEAST SUCCESSFUL EQUAL PAY ADVERTISEMENT

In 1976 the European Economic Community pointed out to the Irish Government that it had not yet implemented the agreed sex equality legislation. The Dublin Government immediately advertised for an equal pay enforcement officer. The advertisement offered different salary scales for men and women.

THE MOST BORING LECTURE

One of the most boring lecturers in the civilised world is certainly Dr David Coward of Leeds University. He won the 'Boring Lecturer of the Year' contest, held annually at Leeds, two years running. Lecturers nominate themselves and may speak on any subject. Dr Coward, a lecturer in the French Department, set the record in 1977 with a delightfully dull talk on 'The problem of the manned urinal'. In winning, he fended off such slight opposition as a man who fell asleep during his third sentence amidst boos and catcalls, and a member of the medical faculty whose lecture 'How to tell right from left' was repeatedly illustrated by slides of a billiard ball viewed from different angles.

The previous year Dr Coward had won with a Marxist explanation of a joke about coconuts. 'It wasn't a terribly good joke,' he said, 'but after I had explained it for twenty minutes people began to see its latent merits.' He retired from the competition undefeated.

THE WORST PREACHER

For sheer creative dullness the Reverend Frederick Denison Maurice (1805–1872) has few equals. Of his sermons Mr Aubrey de Vere said: 'Listening to him was like eating pea soup with a fork'.

Like the members of his congregation, we shall never know what his sermons were about. Sir Mounstuart Grant was one of his most avid fans. 'I must have heard him, first and last, some thirty or forty times, and never carried away one clear idea, or even the impression that he had more the faintest conception of what he himself meant.'

When asked to summarize a Maurice address, Dr Benjamin Jowett, Master of Balliol College, Oxford, replied: 'Well, all that I could make out was that today was yesterday and this world is the same as the next.'

The only serious competition to the Reverend Maurice comes from Dr Robert South who, in 1689, is said to have put his entire congregation to sleep, including the King of England.

At one point he interrupted his sermon to say: 'My Lord Lauderdale, rouse yourself. You snore so loud that you will wake the King.'

THE MOST UNSUCCESSFUL INVENTOR

Between 1962 and 1977 Mr Arthur Paul Pedrick patented 162 inventions, none of which were taken up commercially.

Among his greatest inventions were 'A bicycle with amphibious capacity', spectacles which improved vision in poor visibility and an arrangement whereby a car may be driven from the back seat.

The grandest scheme of Mr Pedrick, who described himself as the 'One-Man-Think-Tank-Basic Physics Research Laboratories of 77 Hillfield Road, Selsey, Sussex', was to irrigate deserts of the world by sending a constant supply of snowballs from the Polar regions through a network of giant peashooters.

He patented several golf inventions – including a golf ball which could be steered in flight – that contravened the rules of the game.

THE LEAST SUCCESSFUL DEMOLITION

Margate Pier was declared dangerous in 1978 after violent gales had lashed the Kent coast. It was thought best to pull the Pier down before it collapsed.

In January 1979 the demolition team arrived and detonated an immense charge of gelignite. The explosion sent water hundreds of feet into the air, but left the Pier's essential character unchanged. After a second 'demolition' a rivet was found embedded in the wall of a seafront pub and police insisted that all future attempts should be made at high tide. The result was that explosion number four took place at midnight and woke up all Margate's sea front.

The demolition team made six further attempts before a Margate councillor suggested that, in view of the large crowds they attracted, the unsuccessful explosions should be made a weekly tourist attraction.

After the fourteenth attempt, the demolition team was retired and a replacement company employed. After attempt number 15, the lifeboat house on the pier was seen to be at a slight angle.

TWO

OFF DUTY

'Tell me, Mr MacMahon, how
long did it take you to learn to
play chess so badly?'
'Sir, it's been nights of study and
self-denial.'
*Conversation during a display match in
Northern Ireland in 1947.*

THE WORST TOURIST

THE WORST PHRASEBOOK

THE WORST VOYAGE

THE WORST DEAF AID

THE LEAST ACCURATELY LABELLED
MUSEUM EXHIBIT

THE LEAST SUCCESSFUL DEFROSTING
DEVICE

THE WORST CAR HIRE SERVICE

THE LEAST SUCCESSFUL TV
PROGRAMME

THE LEAST SUCCESSFUL FIREWORK

Every decision you make is a mistake.
Edward Dahlberg

THE LEAST ACCURATELY LABELLED
MUSEUM EXHIBIT

A first-class example of inaccurate labelling was discovered in October 1971 in County Durham. The object was exhibited in a South Shields museum as a Roman *sestertius* coin, minted between AD 135 and AD 138. However, Miss Fiona Gordon, aged 9, pointed out that it was, in fact, a plastic token given away free by a soft drinks firm in exchange for bottle labels. The dating was, in her view, almost 2,000 years out.

When challenged to provide evidence, she said: 'I knew because the firm's trademark was printed on the back.'

A spokesman for the Roman Fort museum said: 'The token was designed as a Roman replica. The trouble was that we construed the letter "R" on the coin to mean "Roma". In fact it stood for "Robinsons", the soft drink manufacturers.'

THE WORST TOURIST

The least successful tourist on record is Mr Nicholas Scotti of San Francisco. In 1977 he flew from America to his native Italy to visit relatives.

En route the plane made a one-hour fuel stop at Kennedy Airport. Thinking that he had arrived, Mr Scotti got out and spent two days in New York believing he was in Rome.

When his nephews were not there to meet him, Mr Scotti assumed they had been delayed in the heavy Roman traffic mentioned in their letters. While tracking down their address, the great traveller could not help noticing that modernization had brushed aside most, if not all, of the ancient city's landmarks.

He also noticed that many people spoke English with a distinct American accent. However, he just assumed that Americans got everywhere. Furthermore, he assumed it was for their benefit that so many street signs were written in English.

Mr Scotti spoke very little English himself and next asked a policeman (in Italian) the way to the bus depot. As chance would have it, the policeman came from Naples and replied fluently in the same tongue.

After twelve hours travelling round on a bus, the driver handed him over to a second policeman. There followed a brief argument in which Mr Scotti expressed amazement at the Rome police force employing someone who did not speak his own language.

Scotti's brilliance is seen in the fact that even when told he was in New York, he refused to believe it.

To get him on a plane back to San Francisco, he was raced to the airport in a police car with sirens screaming. 'See,' said Scotti to his interpreter, 'I know I'm in Italy. That's how they drive.'

THE LEAST SUCCESSFUL WEEKEND IN PARIS

In 1977 thirty-two Coventry housewives decided to 'pop over to Paris' for the weekend. Such were the delays and disasters encountered that they arrived in the French capital with only two hours to spare before they were due to return home.

One of their number, Mrs Cathleen Fox, said, 'It was ridiculous. We spent all weekend travelling.'

After eight hours on the boat and 15 hours on the coach, the housewives got out to find that they were still 80 miles from Paris. They booked into a hotel at Compiegne where they had to rest three to a room. 'Then a cat wet the bed,' said one of the women, 'and we were six to a room.'

When they eventually got to Paris, they found that the courier couldn't speak French.

After a quick look round, they set off for home. They called at the same hotel where the same cat wet the bed again and also ate their chicken lunch prior to their arrival.

THE WORST PHRASEBOOK

Pedro Carolino is one of the all-time greats. In 1883 he wrote an English–Portuguese phrasebook despite having little or no command of the English language.

His greatly recommended book *The New Guide of the Conversation in Portuguese and English* has now been re-printed under the title *English As She is Spoke*.

After a brief dedication:

'We expect then, who the little book (for the care what we wrote him, and for her typographical correction) that may be worth the acceptation of the studious persons, and especially of the youth, at which we dedicate him particularly'.

Carolino kicks off with some 'Familiar phrases' which the Portuguese holidaymaker might find useful. Among these are

Dress your hairs
This hat go well
Undress you to

Exculpate me by your brother's
She make the prude
Do you cut the hairs?
He has tost his all good

He then moves on to 'Familiar Dialogues' which include 'For to wish the good morning', and 'For to visit a sick'.

Dialogue 18 – 'For to ride a horse' – begins: 'Here is a horse who have bad looks. Give me another. I will not that. He not sall know to march, he is pursy, he is foundered. Don't you are ashamed to give me a jade as like? he is undshoed, he is with nails up'. In the section on 'Anecdotes' Carolino offers the following guaranteed to enthrall any listener:

'One eyed was laied against a man which had good eyes that he saw better than him. The party was accepted. I had gain, over said the one eyed; why I se you two eyes, and you not look me who one'.

It is difficult to top that, but Carolino manages in a useful section of 'Idiotisms and proverbs'. These include:

Nothing some money, nothing of Swiss
He eat to coaches
A take is better than two you shall have
The stone as roll not heap up not foam

and the well-known expression

The dog than bark not bite

Carolino's particular genius was aided by the fact that he did not possess an English–Portuguese Dictionary. However, he did possess Portuguese–French and French–English dictionaries through both of which he dragged his original expressions. The results yield language of originality and great beauty. Is there anything in conventional English which could equal the vividness of 'To craunch a marmoset'?

THE LEAST MYSTERIOUS
MYSTERY TOUR

In 1971 Mr and Mrs William Farmer of Margate travelled to Wales for their summer holidays. At the start of the week they joined a British Rail mystery tour. It took them straight back to Margate. 'We were expecting the Welsh mountains,' they said afterwards.

'We nearly fell through the platform,' said Mr Farmer, who had been looking forward to getting away all the summer. Declining a tour of the town, Mr and Mrs Farmer popped home for a cup of tea.

THE LEAST SUCCESSFUL ROUND
THE WORLD CYCLIST

Mr Michael Murphy, a 22-year-old draftsman from Stevenage in Hertfordshire, set off in August 1975 to cycle round the world. During the next two years he was robbed by Yugoslavian peasants, stoned by tribesmen in the Khyber Pass and nearly froze to death in a blizzard. When he finally arrived back in England in April 1977, he had only to collect his bike at Heathrow Airport and cycle the last 40 miles home. After 25,000 miles he confidently expected to make it back to Stevenage. His hopes were crushed, as was his bicycle, by a conveyor belt joining the plane to the customs hall. He had to hitch a lift home.

THE LEAST SUCCESSFUL
BALLOON FLIGHT

In 1823 Mr Charles Green, the pioneer balloonist, climbed into his basket and lit the take–off fire. The balloon rose slowly, but due to oversight or a practical joke the ropes were inadequately tied. The result was that the basket stayed behind on the ground. Rather than remain in it, Mr Green and a colleague clung on to the balloon hoop. Thus dangling, they floated over Cheltenham.

THE LEAST SUCCESSFUL ATTEMPT
TO MEET A RELATIVE AT AN AIRPORT

In 1975 Mrs Josephine Williams and her family went to meet a long-lost brother at Heathrow Airport. They took home a complete stranger.

Greatly relaxed by in-flight drinking facilities, the traveller wandered into the airport lounge to be smothered by the kisses of Mrs Williams and her sisters. 'Gee, this is great,' he kept saying, all the while cuddling Mrs Williams in a manner which she later described as 'not like a brother'.

His enthusiasm for British hospitality was modified, however, when Mr Williams shook his hand firmly and ushered him to a parked car.

They first suspected that something was amiss when their relative tried to jump out of the car while travelling at speed up the motorway.

When told that he was being taken to a family reunion in Coventry, he replied, 'Take my money. Here's my wallet. Take it and let me go.'

Slumped miserably in the front seat, he added, 'This is the first time I have been to England and I am being kidnapped.'

'I thought from the beginning he wasn't my brother,' Mrs Williams said later, 'but my sisters wouldn't listen. They said I was only twelve when he left for America and wouldn't remember.'

THE WORST VOYAGE

Mr William Smith of Norfolk sailed from Scotland to Great Yarmouth in August 1978 . Showing great independence of mind, en route, he missed Bridlington Harbour by 400 yards and rammed a jetty; at Yarmouth he overshot by 90 miles and ran aground off Kent.

A full-scale search for the boat was hampered by the change in its appearance. When it left Scotland, it was black with one mast. When rescued, it had two masts and was painted green. 'I passed the time while I was aground redecorating', Mr Smith explained.

Entering Yarmouth Harbour, he scraped a floating museum, collided with a small coaster and hit an entrant for the Tall Ships yacht race. He also knocked several guard rails of a trimaran and got the ropes of the cargo vessel *Grippen* wrapped round his mast.

Describing the voyage as 'Pleasant with no hassle or worries', Mr Smith said he planned sailing to Australia next.

THE LEAST SUCCESSFUL NAVIGATOR

Mr Ronald Davies took over two years to make the voyage from Belfast to Plymouth. A duller man would have done it in a few days. He left Ireland in 1974 because the UDA Protestants suspected him of working for the IRA while the IRA suspected him of working for British Intelligence. The situation was clearly impossible and so he set sail with his girlfriend, Brenda Collopy, aiming for the Isle of Man, in their 17-foot sloop, *Calcutta Princess*. In the months which followed they attracted six coastguard alerts, four lifeboat rescues and the assistance of a Royal Navy Helicopter and the aircraft carrier *Hermes*.

On the first leg of their journey, to the Isle of Man, Mr Davies and Miss Collopy got lost and had to be guided into Douglas by a lifeboat. From there they went to Holyhead and set sail for Fishguard. When they failed to arrive the coastguards mounted a search. The mariners eventually appeared in Waterford across the Irish Sea. They set course again for Fishguard but turned up back in Holyhead. On the third attempt they made it to Fishguard.

Later, off the Devon coast, they had to be guided by radio into Clovelly. In Cornish waters their first port of call was Padstow from where they set sail for Newquay. However they were unable to find their way into the harbour and returned to Padstow where they got caught in a storm and had to be rescued by the Padstow lifeboat. At this point Miss Collopy left the boat and Mr Davies carried on alone. After a second rescue by the lifeboat from Padstow five weeks later, he made it as far as the waters off St. Ives where yet again he had to be towed in by lifeboat. He completed the journey overland in August 1977.

THE WORST PROTEST MARCH

On 26 May 1979 the British Communist Party organized a daytrip to Calais for a protest march against the Common Market. There was to have been a mass march through the streets, led by a jazz band, and a reception with M. Jean-Jacques Barthes, the Communist Mayor.

When the 250 British daytrippers arrived at Calais harbour, they heard that the march had been called off because of the rain. They were also told that the jazz band would not be arriving. 'They were too expensive', a tour operator said at the docks, 'and they wanted to bring a piano.'

In any case, it was discovered that the British had left their banner in the coach at Dover and the French would not know what they were demonstrating about. In spite of this, the visitors decided to hold a short march from the lunch room to the meeting hall. However, the lunch venue was changed at the last minute and the hall turned out to be across the road. 'It's not really far enough to march', commented the tour director, Mr Landen Temple.

After the speeches, Mr Temple announced that the mayoral reception was off. Apparently the room had been double booked with a convention of football referees who took precedence.

Furthermore, an international meeting of trade unionists planned for four o'clock had been mistakenly held while the British delegation was having lunch. Also, the social evening with the Calais Young Communists was cancelled because they turned out to be a serious bunch who wanted to have a meeting instead.

'It's been a bit of a mess all round' said Mr Temple with an engaging smile.

THE LEAST SUCCESSFUL ATTEMPT TO SOLVE THE MYSTERY OF THE LOCH NESS MONSTER

All attempts to find the Loch Ness Monster have failed. No one has failed more magnificently than the four Hemel Hempstead firemen who in 1975 tried to seduce it.

Believing that feminine wiles would lure the beast from the deep, they built a thirty-foot long *papier mâché* female monster, equipped with long eyelashes, an outboard motor and a pre-recorded mating call. 'Sex solves everything,' said one of the firemen.

Painted blue and green, the monster then set off in search of romance with two firemen inside steering. They travelled fifteen miles offering flirtation and mystery, but encountered only sustained hormonal indifference from the deep. There are two possible reasons.

First the firemen learned that their pre-recorded mating call was that of a bull walrus and so unlikely to interest the Ness beast.

Second the outboard motor developed a fault during the voyage. The monster went into a flat spin, veered off backwards and crashed prostrate across a jetty.

No girl is at her best under these circumstances.

THE LEAST SUCCESSFUL ATTEMPT TO LIGHT A COAL FIRE

In 1972 Derek Langborne, a scientist from Upton, near Didcot, built a fire in his grate and lit it. He then popped outside to fill the coal scuttle.

When he returned, he observed that, in its enthusiasm

to heat the room, one log had rolled out of the grate and set fire to the log box. He picked it up and carried it out into the garden. On the way out he brushed against a curtain covering the front door. By the time he returned the curtain and the door were both in flames.

While telephoning Didcot Fire Brigade, he noticed that the log box, which he had deposited in the garden, had now set fire to his car.

He then put on his overcoat and approached the car with a bucket of water. In the process he tripped over a partly-filled petrol can.

Seeing that Mr Langborne was in good form, his neighbour called the fire brigade. By the time the fire brigade arrived, Mr Langborne himself was on fire with flames now leaping freely from his overcoat.

THE LEAST SUCCESSFUL
HUNTING PLOY

At the turn of the century Mr Walter Winans, an American millionaire, went deer-stalking in Scotland. Wishing to make his white horse less obstrusive, he decided to paint it black.

To effect the disguise he procured two foul-smelling dyes from a hairdresser and two hogs' hair brushes designed for oil painting purposes.

Winans proclaimed the dye a 'great success' since its foul odour kept the midges off while riding. It also kept off the deer who could smell it coming from miles away.

THE WORST DEAF AID

During a visit to his doctor in March 1978, Mr Harold Senby of Leeds found that his hearing improved when the aid which he had been wearing for the past 20 years was removed. 'With it in I couldn't hear much,' he said. 'But with it out I had almost perfect hearing.'

Closer medical examination revealed that in the 1950s a deaf aid mould was made for his left ear instead of his right. 'Over the years I have been fitted with several new aids, but no one noticed that I had been wearing them in the wrong hole.'

THE SLOWEST SOLUTION OF
A CROSSWORD

On 4 April 1932 *The Times* of London printed its daily crossword.

In May 1966 the paper received a letter from a lady in Fiji announcing that she had just completed it. Thirty-four years will be extremely difficult to beat. Apparently her mother had started it, but tasted defeat over clues like 'Islanders who end in rebellion' (eight letters).

The newspaper then lined a trunk for some years which was the only sensible way to pass the Second World War. It was next found in an English attic by the lady in Fiji's sister who regularly posted crosswords to her puzzle-mad relative.

Over the years she worried away at it – until an 'S' appeared on the end of the rebellious islanders. An initial 'C' followed and a tell tale 'P' became the third letter. 'Cypriots'.

LARGEST NUMBER OF DRIVING
TEST FAILURES

By April 1970 Mrs Miriam Hargrave had failed her test thirty-nine times. In the eight preceding years she had received two hundred and twelve driving lessons at a cost of £300. She set the new record while driving triumphantly through a set of red traffic lights in Wakefield, Yorkshire. Disappointingly, she passed at the fortieth attempt (3 August 1970) but eight years later she showed some of her old magic when she was reported as saying that she still didn't like doing right-hand turns.

THE FASTEST FAILURE OF A
DRIVING TEST

In the early 1970s Mrs Helen Ireland of Auburn in California failed her driving test in the first second.

She got into the car, said 'Good morning' to the tester and started the engine. However, she mistook the accelerator for the clutch and shot straight through the wall of the Driving Test Centre.

[In 1969 an accelerator/clutch confusion enabled Mrs Beatrice Park to drive into the River Wey at Guildford during her fifth test. She and her examiner climbed on to the roof and waited to be rescued. The examiner was later sent home in a state of shock, still clutching his clipboard. When Mrs Park asked if she had passed her test she was told: 'We cannot say until we have seen the examiner's report.']

THE LEAST SUCCESSFUL LION

In 1970 a lion escaped from a circus in Italy. Typically, it found a small boy and started to chase him. Less typically the small boy's mother turned on the lion and badly mauled it. The animal suffered severe head and skin wounds, and received treatment for shock.

THE FASTEST DEFEAT IN CHESS

The big name for us in the world of chess is Gibaud, a French chess master.

In Paris during 1924 he was beaten after only four moves by a Monsieur Lazard. Happily for posterity, the moves are recorded and so chess enthusiasts may reconstruct this magnificent collapse in the comfort of their own homes.

Lazard was black and Gibaud white:

1: P – Q4, Kt – KB3
2: Kt – Q2, P – K4
3: P × P, Kt – Kt5
4: P – K6, Kt – K6/

White then resigns on realizing that a fifth move would involve either a Q – KR5 check or the loss of his queen.

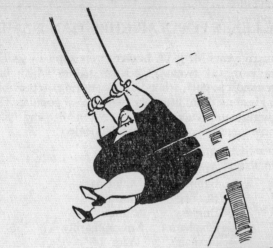

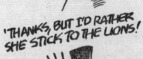

'THANKS, BUT I'D RATHER SHE STICK TO THE LIONS!

THE LEAST POPULAR CHRISTIAN NAMES

For many years Mr J. W. Leaver wrote annually to *The Times* with the twenty Christian names which had proven most popular around the font during the previous year. He at no point listed the twenty least popular. The following names were all used between 1838 and 1900, but now have fallen into spectacular neglect:

Abishag	Ham
Amorous	Lettuce
Babberley	Minniehaha
Brained	Murder
Bugless	Salmon
Clapham	Strongitharm
Despair	Tram
Dozer	Uz
Energetic	Water
Feather	Wonderful

THE LEAST SUCCESSFUL
DEFROSTING DEVICE

The all-time record here is held by Mr Peter Rowlands of
Lancaster whose lips became frozen to his lock in 1979
while blowing warm air on it.

'I got down on my knees to breathe into the lock.
Somehow my lips got stuck fast.'

While he was in the posture, an old lady passed and
inquired if he was all right. 'Alra? Igmmlptk', he replied
at which point she ran away.

'I tried to tell her what had happened, but it came out
sort of . . . muffled,' explained Mr Rowlands, a pottery
designer.

He was trapped for twenty minutes ('I felt a bit fool-
ish') until constant hot breathing brought freedom. He
was subsequently nicknamed 'Hot Lips'.

THE WORST CAR HIRE SERVICE

When David Schwartz left university in 1972, he set up Rent-a-wreck as a joke. Being a natural prankster, he acquired a fleet of beat-up shabby, wreckages waiting for the scrap heap in California.

He put on a cap and looked forward to watching people's faces as he conducted them round the choice of bumperless, dented junkmobiles.

To his lasting surprise there was an insatiable demand for them and he now has 26 thriving branches all over America. 'People like driving round in the worst cars available,' he said. Of course they do.

'If a driver damages the side of a car and is honest enough to admit it, I tell him, "Forget it". If they bring a car back late we overlook it. If they've had a crash and it

SORRY... I THOUGHT YOUR WIFE WAS ONE OF OURS!

doesn't involve another vehicle we might overlook that too.'

'Where's the ashtray?' asked one Los Angeles wife, as she settled into the ripped interior. 'Honey,' said her husband, 'the whole car's the ash tray.'

THE LEAST SUCCESSFUL CAR

Ford produced the car of the decade in 1957 – the Edsel. Half of the models sold proved spectacularly defective. If lucky, you could have got a car with any or all of the following features: doors that wouldn't close, bonnets and boots that wouldn't open, batteries that went flat, hooters that stuck, hubcaps that dropped off, paint that peeled, transmissions that seized up, brakes that failed and push buttons that couldn't be pushed even with three of you trying.

In a stroke of marketing genius, the Edsel, one of the biggest and most lavish cars ever built, coincided with a phase when people increasingly wanted economy cars. As *Time* magazine said: 'It was a classic case of the wrong car for the wrong market at the wrong time.'

Unpopular to begin with, the car's popularity declined. One business writer at the time likened the Edsel's sales graph to an extremely dangerous ski-slope. He added that, so far as he knew, there was only one case of an Edsel ever being stolen.

THE LEAST SATISFACTORY GARAGE

The least satisfactory garage in the history of covered car parking adjoins a semi-detached house at Elkwood, Templelogue in Dublin.

In 1978 prospective buyers of Mr Donal O'Carroll's home were intrigued to see that four concrete steps led up to the garage.

The estate agent handling the sale said, 'I understand the driveway was very steep which was why the steps were put in. The garage is ideal for anyone wanting an extra room, but certainly not if you want to park your car.'

THE WORST AIRCRAFT

Among such craft one holds special place: Count Caproni's Ca 90. Like an immense houseboat with nine multi-layered wings and eight engines, it was launched on Lake Maggiore in January 1921. An Italian historian said it 'would not have looked out of place sailing up the English Channel with the Spanish Armada'.

The test pilot was a Signor Semprini and his nervous doubts were overruled by Count Caproni who ordered him to take off with a ballast load equivalent to sixty passengers.

Semprini revved his 3200 hp engines and rose up off the lake. Monstrously unstable, the nose dipped briefly with the result that the ballast rolled to the front of the plane, the wings snapped and the Ca 90 plunged into the water.

THE LEAST SUCCESSFUL
TV PROGRAMME

In 1978 an opinion poll showed that a French television programme was watched by no viewers at all.

The great day for French broadcasting was 14 August, when not one person saw the extensive interview with an Armenian woman on her fortieth birthday. It ranged over the way she met her husband, her illnesses and the joy of living.

The poll said that 67 per cent had preferred a Napoleonic costume drama and 33 per cent had opted for 'It's a Knockout'.

The programme was transmitted at peak-viewing time and was selected in the previous day's *France Soir* as the best programme on the channel that evening.

THE 'MISS SMILE' WHO WAS
MISERABLE

As part of the 1978 'National Smile Week', Miss Moya Ann Church was voted Miss National Smile Princess.

Only sixty seconds after the 25 year old beauty queen took office, she lost her crown. It was eventually found in a pile of rubbish after an anxious search.

Once found, she smiled with relief. This was the only occasion when she smiled during her entire week of office.

Then a jostling bystander spilled coffee over her 'Smile' sash and £100 dress. Both were ruined.

Next day she locked herself out of her house at Weston-Super-Mare. 'That was bad enough', she said, 'but on Tuesday my car broke down and, when I left it to phone the garage, I got a parking ticket.

'So many things have gone wrong that you have to smile', she said, without smiling. After her final photographic session she missed her train home.

THE MOST UNSUCCESSFUL BROADCAST OF A BEAUTY CONTEST

The most distinctive broadcast of a Miss Great Britain Contest was made by Yorkshire Television in September 1978. The recording of the show started with audience applause and suitable music. Then Mr Tony Monopoly, the compère, bounded on to the stage of the Berengaria Theatre at Morecambe and announced 'Good evening and – sorry, sorry. Have to do it again'. A vision mixer had developed a technical fault and the opening had to be re-recorded. To audience applause and suitable music, Mr Tony Monopoly bounded on again and everything went smoothly, 'Good evening and welcome to the Miss Great Britain Contest coming to you from Morecambe'.

Yorkshire Television, however, broadcast the first version. 'I couldn't believe what I saw', said Mr Laurie Higgins, head of Outside Broadcasts. 'It was an unbelievable clanger and my biggest disaster in 25 years. In fact, the viewers love that sort of thing.'

THE MOST UNSUCCESSFUL
RELIGIOUS PROCESSION

At the end of the sixteenth century regular processions were organized around Hereford Cathedral to mark holy occasions. Before one such, the Dean of Hereford, Dr Price decided that in view of his own importance he would not, as before, walk on foot with the ruck of lowlier canons. He would instead ride on horseback so that he might be more easily seen reading from his prayer book. The proud cleric mounted his mare, opened his book and took to the streets.

His reading was at an early stage when a stallion broke loose, saw his mare and mounted her.

The dean was trapped, read practically nothing and swore he would never ride in a procession again.

THE MOST UNSUCCESSFUL CLAIRVOYANTS

A convention of clairvoyants was held in April 1978 at the Sheraton Hotel in Paris. Readers of palms and tea-cups, tellers of Tarot and gazers into crystal balls turned up in large numbers.

On the last day an English reporter asked if there would be another conference next year. One of the clairvoyants replied: 'We don't know yet'.

THE MOST UNSUCCESSFUL LYING IN STATE

After death, many religions leave dead bishops lying about the church so that mourners may pay their last respects.

The most unsuccessful such event happened in March 1896 at a Greek Orthodox church in Methymni.

After two days' lying in state, clad in episcopal vestments, the Bishop of Lesbos, Nicephorus Glycas, suddenly sat bolt upright, glared at the mourners and asked: 'What are you staring at?'

THE LEAST SUCCESSFUL PSYCHIC ACT

The hypnotist Romark announced in 1977 that he was going to give a public display of his psychic powers. 'I am going to drive a car, blindfold, through Ilford,' he said.

On 12 October he duly placed two coins, a slice of dough and a thick band across his eyes. Shortly afterwards he climbed into a yellow Renault and set off down Cranbrook Road.

After 20 yards he drove confidently into the back of a parked police van. A large admiring crowd formed around our man who later said: 'That van was parked in a place that logic told me it wouldn't be'.

THE LEAST SUCCESSFUL SAINT

Judas Thaddaeus was one of Christ's Apostles and later became known as Saint Jude. For the next eighteen centuries, however, he was entirely ignored. While other saints were invoked daily, hardly a prayer was offered in St Jude's direction: This was largely because he was confused in the public mind with Judas Iscariot who betrayed Christ. This oversight was eventually corrected when the Church made him the Patron Saint of 'Hopeless Cases'.

THE FUNERAL THAT DISTURBED THE CORPSE

Perhaps the most unsuccessful funeral ever held was that of an oriental missionary called Schwartz. The service was held in Delhi at the end of the last century and culminated in the congregation singing the favourite hymn of the recently deceased Dr Schwartz. The mourners were surprised during the final verse to hear a voice from the coffin joining in.

THE LEAST SUCCESSFUL PUB

Between August 1975 and October 1977 the Fox and Goose pub in Birmingham did not serve any beer at all. A special celebration was organised for 31 October 1977 to mark the end of the draymen's strike which had caused the shortage. It was reported that two minutes before opening time on the great day there was a power cut which put the electrically operated beer pumps out of action.

THE WEAKEST BEER EVER BREWED

This was brewed in Germany by Sunner, Colne-Kalk in 1918. It had an original gravity of 1,000.96 degrees and its strength is estimated to be 1/30th of the weakest beer at present available in Britain and America. It was so unpopular with the beer-drinking Germans that it was taken off the market almost immediately.

THE LEAST SUCCESSFUL ALCOHOLICS ANONYMOUS MEETING

A 1974 dinner dance for the Belfast branch of Alcoholics Anonymous ended in a cloakroom brawl after £385 had been spent at the bar.

The manager of the hotel at which the event was held said the trouble was not so much caused by those who had abjured the grape. 'It was their friends.'

THE LEAST SUCCESSFUL FIREWORK

The most unsuccessful firework so far ignited was the
'Fat Man' Roman candle perfected in 1975 by Mr George
Plimpton of New York. It weighed 720 pounds, was
forty inches long and was developed to break the record
for the most spectacular firework ever. It succeeded
admirably.

Lighting it, Mr Plimpton confidently predicted that it
would reach an altitude in excess of 3,000 feet. Instead of
this, however, it hissed, whistled and blew a ten-foot
crater in the earth.

THE MOST UNSUCCESSFUL
FIREWORK DISPLAY

The reign of King James II got off to a fine start when a stately firework display was organised on the River Thames the day after his coronation. As the first one was lit, an over-enthusiastic spark gave premature encouragement to the rest. One of the most spectacular firework collections of the century was gone inside a minute. There was a simultaneous banging and whizzing so great that dozens of spectators jumped into the Thames and for hours afterwards the city of London was full of coachmen chasing their runaway horses.

FAILED ATTEMPTS TO
BREAK RECORDS

In September 1978 Mr Terry Gripton, of Stafford, failed to break the world shouting record by two and a half decibels. 'I am not surprised he failed,' his wife said afterwards. 'He's really a very quiet man and doesn't even shout at me.'

In August of the same year Mr Paul Anthony failed to break the record for continuous organ playing by 387 hours.

His attempt at the Golden Fry Fish Restaurant in Manchester ended after 36 hours 10 minutes, when he was accused of disturbing the peace. 'People complained I was too noisy,' he said.

In January 1976 Mr Barry McQueen failed to walk backwards across the Menai Bridge playing the bagpipes. 'It was raining heavily and my drone got waterlogged,' he said.

A TV cameraman thwarted Mr Bob Specas' attempt to topple 100,000 dominoes at the Manhattan Center, New York, on 9 June 1978. 97,500 dominoes had been set up when he dropped his press badge and set them off.

THREE

LAW AND ORDER

Every man has a scheme that
will not work.
Howe's Law

THE NOISIEST BURGLAR

THE LEAST SUCCESSFUL BANK ROBBER

THE LEAST PROFITABLE ROBBERY

THE WORST GETAWAY

THE LEAST SUCCESSFUL ATTEMPT TO
CATCH A THIEF

THE LEAST SUCCESSFUL POLICE DOGS

THE WORST JURY

THE MOST UNSUCCESSFUL PRISON
ESCAPE

THE WORST PRISON GUARDS

They say best men are moulded
out of faults
And, for the most, become
much more the better
For being a little bad.
Measure For Measure, Act V

THE NOISIEST BURGLAR

A Parisian burglar set new standards for the entire criminal world, when, on 4 November 1933, he attempted to rob the home of an antique dealer. At the time he was dressed in a fifteenth century suit of armour which dramatically limited his chances both of success and escape. He had not been in the house many minutes before its owner was awakened by the sound of clanking metal.

The owner got up and went out on to the landing where he saw the suit of armour climbing the stairs. He straightaway knocked the burglar off balance, dropped a small sideboard across his breastplate, and went off to call the police. Under cross examination a voice inside the armour confessed to being a thief trying to pull off a daring robbery. 'I thought I would frighten him', he said.

Unfortunately for our man, the pressure of the sideboard had so dented his breastplate that it was impossible to remove the armour for 24 hours, during which period he had to be fed through the visor.

THE LEAST SUCCESSFUL DETECTIVE

Detective G. Walsh occupies a special pedestal in the history of sleuths. In August 1797 he pursued William and Dorothy Wordsworth all over the Quantocks in the belief that they were French spies.

An informant had sent him the following note:

'The man (with a woman who passes for his sister) has Camp Stools, which he and his visitors take with them when they go about the country upon their nocturnal or diurnal excursions. They have also a portfolio in which they enter their observations, which they have been heard to say were almost finished.'

We get some idea of Walsh's determination when Coleridge writes: 'He repeatedly hid himself for hours together behind a bank at the seaside (our favourite seat) and overheard our conversation.'

The more Wordsworth jotted notes and observations of local life, the more Walsh's suspicions grew. Eventually, he confronted the local landlord.

'Has he (Wordsworth) not been seen wandering on the hills towards the Channel, and along the shore, with books and papers in his hand; taking charts and maps of the country? . . . Speak out, man! Don't be afraid, you are doing your duty to your King and Government.'

'Why', replied the landlord, 'folks do say, your honour, as how he is a poet, and that he is going to put Quantock and all about here in print.'

THE LEAST WELL-PLANNED ROBBERY

Three thieves at Billericay in Essex gave hours of thought in 1971 to raiding the Post Office in Mountnessing Road.

Among the details which they discovered were the times at which there was most cash and least security guard on the premises. They also invested in masks, guns and a getaway car.

At a pre-arranged time, the Mountnessing gang sped through Billericay and screeched to a halt outside the post office.

It was only when they jumped out of the car and ran towards the building that they discovered the one detail which they had omitted to check.

The Post Office had been closed for twelve years. 'We became a general store in 1959,' said the store's manageress, 76-year-old Mrs Gertrude Haylock. She later remarked: 'I saw these two men running toward the shop with shotguns and I said to my customer, "Here is somebody having a lark." '

Once inside the tiny shop, the raiders pointed their guns at Mrs Haylock and her customer, Mrs Constance Clarke, and demanded the contents of the till.

'I told them we had not taken any money that morning and there was only £6 in the till, so they took that. I should think it was a bit of a disappointment to them.

'They looked so funny dressed up like that. It was just like in a film.'

After the robbers left, the customer fainted on realizing that she had been present at an incident.

THE LEAST SUCCESSFUL FRAUD

A Nigerian labourer explored new areas of fraudulent endeavour in March 1967. While working on a building site in Lagos, he altered his pay cheque from £9-4s-0d to £697,000,090-4s. The fraud was entirely successful right up to the moment when he tried to cash it.

THE LEAST SUCCESSFUL
DIAMOND ROBBERY

A daring gang of diamond thieves stole a van in 1978 expecting to get away with half a million pounds worth of uncut diamonds. A spokesman for the Limerick police said afterwards that the raid was carried out with military precision, but that 'they obviously had completely the wrong information'.

The gang stole the wrong van and got away with two dusters and a sack full of industrial diamonds, which look like sand and have virtually no value on the stolen goods market. It was the second theft of industrial diamonds that week.

'It seems to be a popular pastime in Ireland at the moment', said the policeman. 'Italian criminals blow themselves up and ours rob the wrong vans.'

THE LEAST SUCCESSFUL BLACKMAILER

Mr Monte Shoemaker shot to the top of this league in 1978. Wishing to photograph a solicitor in a compromising position, Mr Shoemaker hid in a bedroom cupboard.

His girlfriend accomplice led the legal expert into the room and Mr Shoemaker waited a couple of minutes for a suitable indiscretion to be arranged. He then burst out, took a photograph and demanded money.

When developed, the photograph showed not a solicitor disrobed, but a refrigerator in the corner of the room.

THE LEAST SUCCESSFUL BANK ROBBER

Not wishing to attract attention to himself, a bank robber in 1969 at Portland, Oregon, wrote all his instructions on a piece of paper rather than shout.

'This is a hold-up and I've got a gun,' he wrote and then held the paper up for the cashier to read.

The bemused bank official waited while he wrote out, 'Put all the money in a paper bag.'

This message was pushed through the grille. The cashier read it and then wrote on the bottom, 'I don't have a paper bag,' and passed it back.

The robber fled.

THE LEAST SUCCESSFUL MUGGING

In 1978 Sussex police launched a hunt for a 'six-foot, dark-haired youth of about 20' who failed to mug a five-foot, 74-year-old grandmother.

The youth sprang upon Mrs Ethel West while she was walking through Chichester Cathedral cloisters. The result should have been a foregone conclusion. Surprisingly, however, when Mrs West grabbed the mugger's wrist, he cried, 'Oh God! Oh no! Stop!'

Encouraged by these pleas, she put him in an arm lock at which the mugger cried, 'Oh no, oh Christ!' and ran away.

'If I hadn't been carrying my shopping, I would really have put him on his back,' said Mrs West who took a course in judo when younger.

'Before my husband died I used to practise throwing him at Christmas,' she explained.

THE LEAST ALERT BURGLAR

A Parisian villain broke into a house at the village of Lachelle in 1964. Once inside he began to feel decidedly peckish and so went in search of the icebox. There he found his favourite cheese which it would have been a shame not to try.

He then found some Bath Oliver biscuits and three bottles of champagne.

After a while he began to feel sleepy and decided that he would lie down and digest his meal in comfort. He was arrested next morning fast asleep upstairs in the spare bedroom.

THE CLUMSIEST BURGLAR

Clumsiness is an important quality in our sort of burglar and in 1978 Mr Christopher Fleming displayed this quality in gratifying abundance. His intention was to break into a Chinese restaurant at Tiverton in Devon via a kitchen window, remove as many notes as possible from the till and leave by the same route.

In a manoeuvre that required breathtaking agility, he climbed through the window, lost his balance and fell into a chip fryer. Covered in grease, he clambered out and dripped his way to the till.

Unable to find any notes, he loaded up with £20 in bulky loose change and, with the grease now congealing, walked out of the restaurant straight into the arms of a policeman.

THE WORST BURGLAR

The history of crime offers few figures less suited to undetected burglary than Mr Philip McCutcheon.

He was arrested for the twentieth time when, after his latest robbery, he drove his getaway car into two parked vans. During this man's appearance at York Crown Court in 1971, the judge gave a rare display of careers' advice from the bench.

Giving our man a conditional discharge, Mr Rodney Percy, the Recorder, said: 'I think you should give burglary up. You have a withered hand, an artificial leg and only one eye. You have been caught in Otley, Leeds, Harrogate, Norwich, Beverley, Hull and York. How can you hope to succeed?

'You are a rotten burglar. You are always being caught.'

THE WORST BANK ROBBERS

In August 1975 three men were on their way in to rob the Royal Bank of Scotland at Rothesay, when they got stuck in the revolving doors. They had to be helped free by the staff and, after thanking everyone, sheepishly left the building.

A few minutes later they returned and announced their intention of robbing the bank, but none of the staff believed them. When, at first, they demanded £5,000, the head cashier laughed at them, convinced that it was a practical joke.

Considerably disheartened by this, the gang leader reduced his demand first to £500, then to £50 and ultimately to 50 pence. By this stage the cashier could barely control herself for laughter.

Then one of the men jumped over the counter and fell awkwardly on the floor, clutching at his ankle. The other two made their getaway, but got trapped in the revolving doors for a second time, desperately pushing the wrong way.

THE LEAST PROFITABLE ROBBERY

Intending to steal cash from a supermarket in 1977, a Southampton thief employed a unique tactic to divert the till girl's attention. His method was to collect a trolley full of goods, arrive at her till and put down £10 by way of payment. She would then take the money and open the till, upon which he would snatch the contents.

He arrived at the cash desk and put down the £10. She took it and opened the till; but there was only £4.37 in it.

86

Undeterred, the Southampton thief snatched that and made his getaway, having lost £5.63 on the raid.

The till girl was considerably uncertain what to do for the best. She screamed briefly until calmed by her friend Betty.

THE WORST MOMENT FOR A CRIME

Choosing the right moment is vitally important in any crime. Mr David Goodall of Barnsley, for example, set off in January 1979 to do a bit of shoplifting. He had hardly entered Barnsley's British Home Stores when he was simultaneously seized by eight pairs of hands. The shop was holding a convention of store detectives at the time.

THE WORST GETAWAY

Some admirers claim that the world's worst getaway was executed at Detroit in 1970 by two bank robbers who rushed out into the street to find that their getaway car had been stolen; but this was mere luck and involved no skill on their part at all. How different was the case of the 'Perivale Two'.

In July 1978 Mr Noel Murray and Mr Andrew O'Connor met with total success in robbing the Co-operative Store at Perivale in Middlesex. They burst into the shop, grabbed money bags containing £4,500 and fled to their getaway car.

Thus far they are of no interest to us at all, but then Mr O'Connor, the driver, jumped behind the steering wheel, turned the ignition key the wrong way and jammed the lock. The two then scrambled into another car and did exactly the same thing again, bending the key beyond use.

At the Old Bailey hearing, the prosecuting counsel said that in any case the getaway cars were positioned in the wrong direction. Had they started them, the Perivale Two would have driven straight into the police station.

THE LEAST SUCCESSFUL ACT OF PUBLIC BRAVERY

Occasionally a member of the public steps in bravely to prevent crime. In July 1978 bank employees at Sherman Oaks in California thought they had outwitted a robber when they refused to handle his suspicious package.

Relieved staff watched as the bandit sprinted out of the bank to dump his parcel. However, a man, who was standing outside the bank, saw the robber escaping and chased after him. He tackled the man and returned the package, which, in fact, contained tear gas timed to explode in two minutes, to the bank. It took thirty minutes to clear the air.

THE LEAST SUCCESSFUL ATTEMPT TO CATCH A THIEF

During 1978 a persistent thief had stolen £10 nightly from a newsagent's shop in Barking, Essex. Every morning cash was missing from the till and so the shop-keeper devised a plan to catch the culprit.

Into his shop the owner transported a giant cardboard box which he placed unostentatiously in the middle of the floor. After five o'clock closing, he climbed into the box wherein he spent the entire night.

Nothing stirred until 14 hours later when the excellent sleuth, tired and stiff, emerged at dawn to answer a call of nature. Minutes later he returned, stretching a leg here and rubbing a neck there, to discover that, in his absence, the thief had been, taken £10 from the till, and gone again.

THE CRIMES THAT WERE EASIEST TO DETECT

Any act of genius is marked by a dazzling simplicity. There is about it a logic and inevitability that is deeply satisfying. The following crimes were detected almost immediately after they had been committed.

In 1972 Mr J. Egan from London stole a barge on the River Thames and was very soon caught. There was a dock strike on and his was the only craft moving that day.

Mr J. Ealey committed a burglary in Detroit in 1968 and left his dog at the scene of the crime. The police soon arrived and shouted 'home boy'. They then followed the dog back to the burglar's house. And arrived only seconds after he did.

In May 1976 Vernon Drinkwater and Raymond Heap of Blackburn were accused of stealing a car while trying to sell it to its original owner.

THE LEAST SUCCESSFUL SECRET CAMERA

Attempting to catch a persistent thief in 1978, the Doncaster police set up a secret camera in the changing rooms of a local squash club.

When they played back the film, the police found that all they had succeeded in filming was one of their own policemen wandering round naked and looking for his clothes, which had been stolen.

THE LEAST SUCCESSFUL POLICE DOGS

America has a very strong candidate in 'La Dur', a fearsome looking schnauzer hound, who was retired from the Orlando police force in Florida in 1978. He consistently refused to do anything which might ruffle or offend the criminal classes.

His handling officer, Rick Grim, had to admit: 'He just won't go up and bite them. I got sick and tired of doing that dog's work for him.'

The British contenders in this category, however, took things a stage further. 'Laddie' and 'Boy' were trained as detector dogs for drug raids. Their employment was terminated following a raid in the Midlands in 1967.

While the investigating officer questioned two suspects, they patted and stroked the dogs who eventually fell asleep in front of the fire. When the officer moved to arrest the suspects, one dog growled at him while the other leapt up and bit his thigh.

THE WORST JURY

A murder trial at Manitoba in February 1978 was well advanced, when one juror revealed that he was completely deaf and did not have the remotest clue what was happening.

The judge, Mr Justice Solomon, asked him if he had heard any evidence at all and, when there was no reply, dismissed him.

The excitement which this caused was only equalled when a second juror revealed that he spoke not a word of English. A fluent French speaker, he exhibited great surprise when told, after two days, that he was hearing a murder trial.

The trial was abandoned when a third juror said that he suffered from both conditions, being simultaneously unversed in the English language and nearly as deaf as the first juror.

The judge ordered a retrial.

THE LEAST SUCCESSFUL HANDCUFFING

The most exciting case of handcuff difficulties was reported in the *New Statesman* in 1978. It arose while a British circuit judge was trying a burglar in whose possession a pair of handcuffs had been found.

'I thought' said the judge, 'that the jury might be interested to know how handcuffs could be used to incapacitate a victim.'

Brushing aside the protests of the prosecuting council, he clasped one handcuff around his left wrist. 'And now', he said, 'if I take the other handcuff . . . Oh do be quiet Mr Smith (addressed to the agitated prosecutor) I am going to show the jury how these things work.'

Only when the judge was completely fettered did he learn that the police had not yet recovered the keys. The hearing was adjourned while the judge was led off to the tender mercies of the local blacksmith.

THE LEAST SUCCESSFUL EXECUTIONS

History has furnished us with two executioners worthy of attention. The first performed in Sydney in Australia. In 1803 three attempts were made to hang a Mr Joseph Samuels. On the first two of these the rope snapped, while on the third Mr Samuels just hung there peacefully until he and everyone else got bored. Since he had proved unsusceptible to capital punishment, he was reprieved.

The most important British executioner was Mr James Berry who tried three times in 1885 to hang Mr John Lee at Exeter Jail, but on each occasion failed to get the trap door open.

In recognition of this achievement, the Home Secretary commuted Lee's sentence to 'life' imprisonment. He was released in 1917, emigrated to America and lived until 1933.

THE WORST PRISON GUARDS

The largest number of convicts ever to escape simultaneously from a maximum security prison is 124. This record is held by Alcoente Prison, near Lisbon in Portugal.

During the weeks leading up to the escape in July 1978 the prison warders had noticed that attendances had fallen at film shows which included 'The Great Escape', and also that 220 knives and a huge quantity of electric cable had disappeared. A guard explained: 'Yes, we were planning to look for them, but never got around to it.' The warders had not, however, noticed the gaping holes in the wall because they were 'covered with posters'. Nor did they detect any of the spades, chisels, water hoses and electric drills amassed by the inmates in large quantities. The night before the breakout one guard had noticed that of the 36 prisoners in his block only 13 were present. He said this was 'normal' because inmates sometimes missed roll-call or hid, but usually came back the next morning.

'We only found out about the escape at 6.30 the next morning when one of the prisoners told us,' a warder said later. The searchlights were described as 'our worst enemy' because they had been directed at the warders faces, dazzled them and had made it impossible to see anything around the prison walls. When they eventually checked, the prison guards found that exactly half of the gaol's population was missing. By way of explanation the Justice Minister, Dr Santos Pais, claimed that the escape was 'normal' and part of the 'legitimate desire of the prisoner to regain his liberty.'

THE MOST UNSUCCESSFUL PRISON ESCAPE

After weeks of extremely careful planning, seventy-five convicts completely failed to escape from Saltillo Prison in Northern Mexico. In November 1975 they had started digging a secret tunnel designed to bring them up at the other side of the prison wall.

On 18 April 1976, guided by pure genius, their tunnel came up in the nearby courtroom in which many of them had been sentenced. The surprised judges returned all 75 to jail.

FOUR

PLAYING THE GAME

And the last shall be first.
St Matthew, Ch.19, V.30

THE MOST UNSUCCESSFUL
ANGLING CONTEST

THE WORST ANGLER

THE WORST HOMING PIGEON

THE LEAST SUCCESSFUL GOLF CLUB

THE WORST BOXER

THE WORST SAVE

THE LEAST SUCCESSFUL
CRICKET MATCH

THE WORST MATADOR

THE WORST BET

THE LEAST SUCCESSFUL JOCKEY

Nice Guys come last.
Amos Alonzo Stagg

THE LEAST SUCCESSFUL
PIGEON RACE

One great appeal of this sport is that during the race itself all you have to do is go home and wait.

Even under these ideal conditions, races can still go wrong. One of the most unsuccessful ever was held in 1978, when 6,745 racing pigeons were released at Preston in Lancashire. Of these 5,545 were never seen again.

'In all my forty years with racing pigeons,' said Mr James Paterson, secretary of the Ayrshire Federation of Homing Pigeons, 'I have never known anything like it. They have vanished. Someone suggested they might have flown over a grouse moor and been shot. I can't believe they could have got all 5,545.'

The most likely-sounding explanation was advanced by Mr Tony Soper, the naturalist. He said the birds may have gone to the Devonshire seaside, which sounds a very sensible thing to do.

THE WORST HOMING PIGEON

This historic bird was released in Pembrokeshire in June 1953 and was expected to reach its base that evening.

It was returned by post, dead, in a cardboard box, eleven years later from Brazil. 'We had given it up for lost,' its owner said.

THE MOST UNSUCCESSFUL ANGLING CONTEST

This fine event occurred during the National Ambulance Servicemen's Angling Championship held at Kidderminster in 1972.

Two hundred ambulancemen gathered along the nearby canal and took part in five hours of keenly competitive fishing. In this time not one of them caught anything.

They would still be there now had not a passer-by – after watching them for some minutes – informed them that all the fish had been moved to other waters three weeks before.

THE WORST ANGLER

Thomas Birch, the eighteenth-century scholar, was a keen fisherman. However, he rarely caught anything and so decided to disguise himself in order to lull the fish into a false sense of security.

He constructed an outfit which made him look like a tree. His arms fitted into the branches and his eyes peered through knots in the bark.

Thus attired, he set off down the river bank and took up his position. He still did not catch anything, attracting only suspicious dogs and friends who used to picnic at his feet.

THE HIGHEST EVER SCORE FOR A SINGLE GOLF HOLE

In 1912 an American enthusiast made golfing history, when she took 166 strokes over a 130-yard hole.

During the qualifying round of the Shawnee Invitational for Ladies at Shawnee-on-Delaware, Pennsylvania, she confidently approached the sixteenth hole for which four strokes were normally adequate. Her first shot, however, sent the ball into the Binniekill River, an obstacle which many would regard as final.

When she saw that it floated she boarded a rowing boat, with her husband at the oars and herself at the prow, wielding a golf club. For one and a half miles her husband rowed and kept count of the occasions upon which she had cause to swipe at it.

Eventually, she beached the thing and made her way back through a forest. Fellow competitors had given up hope of ever seeing her again, when they heard the cry of 'fore' and saw the ball fly on the green from a totally unexpected direction. She completed the hole in just under two hours.

'TRY A NUMBER 5 ROD!'

THE BRITISH OPEN: WORST ENTRANT

For 121 years the British Open Golf Championship held no interest for us whatever. But then in July 1976, Mr Maurice Flitcroft, a 46-year-old crane driver from Barrow-in-Furness, changed that.

This fine sportsman, who had never before played a full 18 holes of golf, made history by taking a record 121 strokes in the first qualifying round at Formby in Lancashire.

So upset were the championship committee, when they heard this that they refunded the £30 entry fees to the two golfers drawn to play with him.

'I enjoyed the game', he said afterwards, 'It was good practice'.

THE LEAST SUCCESSFUL GOLF CLUB

The City Golf Club in London is unique among such organizations in not possessing a golf course, ball, tee, caddy or bag. Its whole premises just off Fleet Street do not contain a single photograph of anything that approaches a golfing topic.

'We had a driving range once,' the commissionaire said, 'but we dropped that years ago.' The membership now devotes itself exclusively to eating and drinking.

THE WORST BOXER

Ralph Walton was knocked out in 10½ seconds in a bout at Lewiston, Maine, U.S.A., on 29 September 1946. It happened when Al Couture struck him as he was still adjusting his gum shield in his corner. The 10½ seconds includes 10 seconds while he was counted out.

THE WORST BOXING DEBUT

In February 1977 Mr Harvey Gartley became the first boxer to knock himself out after 47 seconds of the first round of his first fight before either boxer had landed a punch.

It happened in the regional bantamweight heats of the 15th annual Saginaw Golden Gloves contest in Michigan, when Gartley was matched against Dennis

Outlette. Neither boxer had fought in public before. Both were nervous.

Gartley started promisingly and came out of his corner bobbing, weaving and dancing. As the crowd roared them on, Gartley closed in, threw a punch, missed and fell down exhausted. The referee counted him out.

THE WORST SOCCER MATCH

In 1973 Oxbarn Social Club football team arranged a friendly match in Germany. It was an opportunity for the lads, who play in the Wolverhampton Sunday League, to get a holiday abroad and also to meet some new opposition. Only when they entered their opponents' luxury stadium did they realize that they had mistakenly arranged a friendly with a top German first division side. For their part, SVW Mainz were expecting to play Wolverhampton Wanderers, then one of the strongest teams in Britain.

The Oxbarn Club secretary said, 'I thought it looked posh, and when I heard the other side were on an £80 bonus to win, I said to myself, "Something is wrong." '

After the fifteenth goal whistled into Oxbarn's net, their goalkeeper was seen to fall on to his knees. He seemed to be praying for the final whistle. It was around this time that the sixteenth and seventeenth were scored.

Naturally, the Mainz crowd were delighted to watch a team like Oxbarn instead of the mighty Wolverhampton Wanderers. 'They behaved very well,' said the Oxbarn secretary. 'Whenever we got the ball they gave a prolonged cheer.'

Oxbarn Social Club lost 21–0.

THE SMALLEST SOCCER CROWD

The football match which has attracted fewest supporters was that great game between Leicester City and Stockport County on 7 May 1921. It pulled a crowd of 13. This glorious indifference was accentuated by the fact that both teams were playing away from home. Stockport's ground had been temporarily closed and the match was held at Manchester United's immense stadium.

THE WORST SAVE

This honour falls to Senhor Isadore Irandir of the Brazilian team Rio Preto who let in a goal after three seconds.

From the kick off in the soccer match between Corinthians and Rio Preto at Bahia Stadium, the ball was passed to Roberto Rivelino who scored instantly with a left-foot drive from the halfway line. The ball went past the ear of Senhor Irandir, while he was on his knees finishing pre-match prayers in the goalmouth.

THE LEAST SUCCESSFUL
CRICKET MATCH

At the turn of the century, grown men were put to shame by two schoolboy teams in Cambridge. The match brought together King's College Choir School and the Trophy Boys XI.

Trophy Boys won the toss, batted first and were all out

for nought. Then King's went in and Trophy's first ball was a 'no ball'.

This gave the King's Choir school a score of one and victory in the match.

THE LOWEST SCORE IN A TEST MATCH

New Zealand achieved this unique honour in March 1955 when they scored a spectacular 26 against England at Auckland.

It is worth listing the score of the eleven great batsmen who shared the glory.

J. G. Leggatt	1
M. B. Poore	0
B. Sutcliffe	11
J. R. Reid	1
G. O. Rathbone	7
S. N. McGregor	1
H. B. Cave	5
A. R. MacGibbon	0
I. A. Colquhoun	0
A. M. Moir	0 (not out)
J. A. Hayes	0
Extras	0
	26

Sadly, the dismal England side did not enter into the spirit of things, and won by an innings and 20 runs.

OXFORD AND CAMBRIDGE BOAT RACE SINKINGS

After 150 years the honours are shared. Cambridge pioneered the art in 1857, but Oxford showed their mettle in 1925 and again in 1951. The most recent demonstration was by Cambridge in 1978.

The greatest ever Oxford and Cambridge boat race was held in 1912. Both crews sank. Oxford rowed into an early lead but their boat was soon taking water on board. 'We decided', said the cox, H. Bensley-Wells, 'to make for the river bank'.

Once there they all hopped out, upturned the boat and hopped back in again. At this moment, one of their oarsmen saw a friend and disappeared into the crowd for a chat. His colleagues sat in the boat wondering where he was. 'I spotted a chum called Boswell', he told the disbelieving crew on his return.

The cox explained to him that they were actually having a race, if he wouldn't mind getting in. The oarsman expressed no objection, said 'goodbye' to Boswell and jumped in.

No sooner were they waterborne again than they saw the Cambridge crew go past. They were, however, swimming as their boat was underwater.

By this time the Thames was full of boats and crew members. Rescue boats appeared and the race was abandoned.

THE LEAST SUCCESSFUL RUGBY FORWARD

The most tries scored by a rugby player is 250. Our man, however, is Oliver Jones, who scored only three tries in forty-five years of regular playing for the Old Edwardian Exiles.

The silver-haired prop forward scored his third try on 15 October 1966 when he was sixty. 'There was a bit of a scramble on the line,' he said. 'I just dropped on the ball. Nothing spectacular.'

Afterwards there was much back-slapping but Jones didn't let himself go with manly songs and drunken toasts. 'I had to go to my sister's party,' he said.

He used to play rugby because he 'couldn't think of anything else to do on a Saturday.'

THE WORST MATADOR

Raphael Gomez was one of those rare matadors in whose company a bull was often safer than in the hands of a vet. Once when asked what he did to train, he replied 'smoke Havana cigars'.

Known as 'El Gallo', he would stride into the ring manfully, throw a flower at a local beauty and then dedicate the bull to her in a long and florid speech. 'To thee alone I dedicate the life of this bull,' he would say before turning round to strike a fine pose and await the opposition. As soon as it snorted into sight, El Gallo would regularly drop his cape, sprint across the ring and dive headlong over the barrier in a move known technically as the 'Espantada'. 'All of us artists have bad days,' the unique matador used to say. He was sometimes panic stricken simply because of the way a bull looked at him. Ernest Hemingway said that for a bull to kill El Gallo would be 'in bad taste'.

He was brought out of retirement seven times by popular demand. In his last fight on 10 October 1918 El Gallo dedicated the bull to no less than three dignitaries in his longest ever speech and, after all this, he refused to kill it because it had winked at him. Eventually his brother had to kill it to save the family honour.

THE WORST BULLFIGHT

In 1958 the town of Lindsay held a bullfight at which no bulls were killed and no matadors were present.

Since it was Canada's first ever bullfight, six bulls had to be specially imported from Mexico. When they arrived they were suffering from ticks and had to be quarantined for a week. During this time the hired bull-fighters returned home to Mexico.

Next the Ontario Society for the Prevention of Cruelty to Animals ruled that no-one would be allowed to kill the bulls, but that you could win by symbolically tapping them between the shoulder blades. This caused further problems because no-one knew how to corral the maddened bull afterwards.

The second bull kept organizers, local police and stand-in matadors busy for over an hour, while fans shouted encouragement and advice from the stands. Said Police Inspector Gordon Ebert: 'The bull simply refused to co-operate.'

THE LEAST SUCCESSFUL JOCKEY

Few jockeys have been more regularly parted from their horse than the Duc of Alburquerque.

In 1963 he made racing history when bookies offered odds of 66-1 against his finishing the Grand National on horseback. Dividing his time equally between the saddle and the stretcher, this Spanish aristocrat entered the National seven times with consistently impressive results. Generally, he would start with the others, gallop briefly and then wake up in the intensive care unit of the Royal Liverpool Infirmary. It was the fences that caused the trouble.

In 1952 the Duc fell at the sixth fence and almost broke his neck. In 1963 it was the fourth. In 1965 his horse collapsed and in 1973 his stirrup broke. He clung on bravely for eight fences before being sent into inevitable orbit.

In 1974 he fell off during training and staff at the casualty unit were surprised to see him wheeled in before the race had even begun. Undeterred, this fine man rode in the National with a broken collar-bone and a leg in plaster.

'I sat like sack of potatoes,' he said in his faltering English, 'and gave horse no help.' This may explain how he came to complete the course for the only time in his splendid career.

THE WORST BET

Just before the First World War Mr Horatio Bottomley, the British politician and horse owner, carefully devised what he considered to be a sure way of winning a fortune.

His plan was beautifully simple: prior to a race at Blankenberghe in Belgium, he bought all six horses entered. He then hired six English jockeys who were given strict instructions as to the order in which they should cross the finishing line. Leaving nothing to chance, Bottomley backed all the horses, as a final precaution.

All was going smoothly until half way through the race, when a thick sea mist blew inshore and engulfed the whole course. Jockeys could not see each other and judges could not see the horses, and those that finished at all did so in a hopeless jumble.

Mr Bottomley lost a fortune.

FIVE

THE CULTURAL SIDE OF THINGS

It's awful. You'll like it.
Cabaret

THE WORST SINGER

THE WORST SONG ENTRY

THE WORST LINES OF VERSE

THE WORST AMERICAN POET

THE SLOWEST-SELLING BOOK

THE MOST UNSUCCESSFUL VERSION
OF THE BIBLE

'MAN FROM PORLOCK': A TRIBUTE

THE LEAST SUCCESSFUL DISPLAY
OF A PAINTING

THE WORST DRESSED
ROYAL SCULPTURES

THE LEAST SUCCESSFUL
FILM SCREENING

And now, kind friends, what I have
wrote, I hope you will pass o'er.
And not criticize as some have done
hitherto herebefore.

Julia Moore

THE WORST SINGER

The glory of the human voice has never had fuller expression than in the career of Florence Foster Jenkins.

La Jenkins was not apologetically low key in her badness, she was defiantly and gloriously dreadful. No one, before or since, has succeeded in liberating themselves quite so completely from the shackles of musical notation. Opera was her medium and she squawked heroically through the best known arias with a refreshing abandon.

From her birth in Pennsylvania in 1864 to her debut 40 years later, it is fair to say that neither her parents nor her husband gave the slightest encouragement to her musical ambitions.

Then papa left her his fortune and, with this new-found wealth and freedom, she launched her assault upon the musical world.

Her flair for dress design fully equalled her singing gift and, in any concert, thrilled audiences were treated to a minimum of three costume changes. One minute she would appear sporting an immense pair of wings to render 'Ave Maria'. The next she would emerge in the garb of a señorita, with a rose between her teeth and a basket full of flowers to unload her Spanish show stopper, 'Cavelitos'.

In this song she would punctuate each verse by hurling rosebuds into the audience. Once she hurled the basket as well.

The audience could always tell when she was going to grant an encore. She would dispatch her overworked accompanist Cosme McMoon out into the auditorium to collect up the flowers so that she might repeat her triumph.

On 26 October 1944, she hired and filled to capacity the Carnegie Hall in New York for her farewell appearance. She started disappointingly with three correct notes, but her admirers need not have feared. Before long she abandoned pitch, stave, and key and was as out of tune as it is possible to be without coming back in tune again.

THE WORST LINES OF VERSE

For a start, we can rule out James Grainger's promising line:

> 'Come, muse, let us sing of rats.'

Grainger (1721–67) did not have the courage of his convictions and deleted these words on discovering that his listeners dissolved into spontaneous laughter the instant they were read out.

No such reluctance afflicted Adam Lindsay Gordon (1833–70) who was inspired by the subject of war.

> 'Flash! flash! bang! bang! and we blazed away,
> And the grey roof reddened and rang;
> Flash! flash! and I felt his bullet flay
> The tip of my ear. Flash! bang!'

By contrast, Cheshire cheese provoked John Armstrong (1709–79):

> '. . . that which Cestria sends, tenacious paste
> of solid milk . . .'

While John Bidlake was guided by a compassion for vegetables:

> 'The sluggard carrot sleeps his day in bed,
> The crippled pea alone that cannot stand.'

George Crabbe (1754–1832) wrote:

> 'And I was ask'd and authorized to go
> To seek the firm of Clutterbuck and Co.'

William Balmford explored the possibilities of religious verse:

'So 'tis with Christians, Nature being weak
While in this world, are liable to leak.'

And William Wordsworth showed that he could do it if he really tried when describing a pond:

'I've measured it from side to side;
Tis three feet long, and two feet wide.'

For those who like their poetry unmarred by insight and euphony 'The Stuffed Owl: An Anthology of Bad Verse' by Charles Lee and D. B. Wyndham Lewis is highly recommended.

THE WORST MUSICAL TRIO

There are few bad musicians who have a chance to give a recital at a famous concert hall while still learning the rudiments of their instrument. This happened about thirty years ago to the son of a Rumanian gentleman who was owed a personal favour by Georges Enesco, the celebrated violinist. Enesco agreed to give lessons to the son who was quite unhampered by great musical talent.

Three years later the boy's father insisted that he gave a public concert. 'His aunt said that nobody plays the violin better than he does. A cousin heard him the other day and screamed with enthusiasm.' Although Enesco feared the consequences, he arranged a recital at the Salle Gaveau in Paris. However, nobody bought a ticket since the soloist was unknown.

'Then you must accompany him on the piano,' said the boy's father, 'and it will be a sell out.'

Reluctantly, Enesco agreed and it was. On the night an excited audience gathered. Before the concert began Enesco became nervous and asked for someone to turn his pages.

In the audience was Alfred Cortot, the brilliant pianist, who volunteered and made his way to the stage.

The soloist was of uniformly low standard and next morning the music critic of *Le Figaro* wrote: 'There was a strange concert at the Salle Gaveau last night. The man whom we adore when he plays the violin played the piano. Another whom we adore when he plays the piano turned the pages. But the man who should have turned the pages played the violin.'

THE WORST ORCHESTRA

The worst orchestra ever to perform in public was the Portsmouth Symphonia. Formed in 1970, two thirds of its members had never touched an instrument before.

This factor above all others made their renderings of the light classics so refreshingly original. Unhampered by preordained melody, the orchestra tackled the great compositions, agreeing only on when they should start and finish. The cacophony which resulted was naturally an immense hit and before long they made two long playing records. These became very popular, demonstrating yet again the public's great appreciation of incompetence. Leonard Bernstein said that the Portsmouth Symphonia changed his attitude to the William Tell Overture for ever.

THE LEAST SUCCESSFUL CONDUCTING

Although he composed a few symphonies, Hector Berlioz is mainly notable for conducting a concert from which the orchestra left before the end.

It was a rule at the Theatre Italien that musicians did not have to stay beyond midnight. Five to twelve approached and, due to the evening's exquisite chaos, only three-quarters of the ambitiously long programme had been completed.

The clock chimed twelve. Berlioz turned to conduct the last work, his own *Symphonie Fantastique,* and found that only five violins, two violas, four cellos and a trombone remained.

The delighted audience clamoured for them to play the

symphony anyway, but Berlioz explained that this was not possible with five violins, two violas, four cellos and a trombone. 'It is not my fault,' he said in one of the great quotations of musical history. 'The orchestra has disappeared.'

THE LEAST SUCCESSFUL PIANO RECITAL

Early in the 1970s a promising American pianist gave a concert in the chamber music room of the Erewan Hotel in Bangkok. The recital was only a few minutes old when the artist discovered that due to the climate's excessive humidity the D key of the treble clef began to stick repeatedly. As luck would have it, his programme comprised Bach's D minor Toccata and Fugue and his Prelude and Fugue in D major.

The reviewer in the *Bangkok Post* also noted that there was a problem with the piano stool which had been so enthusiastically greased that during one of the more vigorous sections the pianist suddenly found himself swivelling round to face the audience.

Abandoning the Toccata in D minor, he moved on to Liszt's Fantasia in G minor, at which point the G key of the bass clef also stuck. To try and free the notes the virtuoso started kicking the lower section of the piano with his foot with the result that the piano's right leg soon gave way and the whole instrument tilted through 35 degrees.

At this point he rose, bowed and left the stage to audience applause. When he returned he had in his hand a fire axe with which he began to demolish the piano.

On hearing the resounding crash which followed the

ushers came rushing in, and, with the help of the hotel manager, two watchmen and a passing policeman, finally succeeded in disarming the man and dragging him off stage.

THE LEAST SUCCESSFUL SONG WRITER

For twenty years Mr Geoffrey O'Neill has been writing what he calls 'good catchy tunes that people remember and whistle'. In this time he has composed 501 songs and three musicals. Not one of them has been recorded, published or performed by professionals.

Mr O'Neill, who comes from Great Dunmow in Essex, files all his songs away in case there should be a sudden demand for them. He cheerfully reports that song number 102 is called 'Try, Try Again', while number 332 is entitled 'People Think I'm Stupid'. An oil firm employee, he gives public lectures on how unsuccessful his songs are.

THE WORST RECORD

One of the most popular LPs of 1978 was *The World's Worst Record Show* which brought together 30 of the worst pop songs ever recorded.

Three of the tracks were by Jess Conrad. One of them, *Cherry Pie,* is concerned with likening his loved one to a fruit-filled pastry. Another asks *Why am I living?* to an insistent backing of 'wo dah dah yip yip'.

In the barely comprehensible *Transfusion,* Nervous Norvus records his continuing debt to blood donors in the light of his predilection for speeding.

The most reassuringly pointless song is Steve Bent's *I'm going to Spain.* Accompanied by maracas he gives musical justification for his holiday plans revolving around the fact that 'Cousin Norman had a real fine time last year.'

The worst is the contribution by the Legendary Stardust Cowboy who yells, screams, bawls, howls, bays, whoops, yelps, shouts and wails without one word ever being comprehensible, until drowned out by demonic drum and trumpet solos which defy description, all under the name of 'Paralyzed'.

Naturally, the LP was a great hit and sold 25,000 copies a week in the London area alone.

THE WORST SONG ENTRY

Singing an entrancingly drab number called 'Mile after Mile', a Norwegian pop singer, Mr Jan Teigan, scored nil in the 1978 Eurovision Song Contest. The voting from the panels all over Europe was unanimous:

'Norway – no points
        – nul points
        – keine Pünkte'

Next morning the papers were naturally full of Mr Teigan, pushing mention of the actual winner, Izhar Cohen, into a subsidiary paragraph. After the contest press photographers had crowded round our hero giving him star treatment. 'This was my greatest success,' he said, 'I have done what no-one ever did before me. I'm the first Norwegian to get zero points. After the concert I had to make 60 splits for the photographers and I've got lots of offers for TV appearances, tours and interviews. I've never known as much interest taken in me.'

THE WORST BRITISH POET

With William Topaz McGonagall, we approach one of the giants in our field. He was so giftedly bad that he backed unwittingly into genius. Combining a minimal feel for the English language with a total lack of self-awareness and nil powers of observation, he became a poet.

Sitting in his back room in Paton's Lane, Dundee, wishing he was on holiday, he was seized with a desire to write poetry. He paced the room, saying, 'But I know nothing about poetry.' Thus qualified he sat down and penned his first great work.

An Address to the Rev George Gilfillan

All hail to the Rev George Gilfillan of Dundee,
He is the greatest preacher I did ever hear or see.
He is a man of genius bright,
And in him his congregation does delight,
Because they find him to be honest and plain,
Affable in temper, and seldom known to complain.
He preaches in a plain straightforward way,
The people flock to hear him night and day,
And hundreds from the doors are often turn'd away,
Because he is the greatest preacher of the present
    day.

He has written the life of Sir Walter Scott,
And while he lives he will never be forgot,
Nor when he is dead,
Because by his admirers it will be often read;
And fill their minds with wonder and delight,
And wile away the tedious hours on a cold winter's
    night.
He has also written about the Bards of the Bible,
Which occupied nearly three years in which he was
    not idle,
Because when he sits down to write he does it with
    might and main,
And to get an interview with him it would be almost
    vain,
And in that he is always right,
For the Bible tells us whatever your hands findeth to
    do,
Do it with all your might.
Rev George Gilfillan of Dundee, I must conclude
    my muse,
And to write in praise of thee my pen does not
    refuse,
Nor does it give me pain to tell the world fearlessly,
    that when
You are dead they shall not look upon your like
    again.

On one famous occasion, he read this and other of his poems in a pub. 'It was a great triumph. The publican told the waiter to throw a wet towel at me, which, of course, the waiter did and I received the wet towel, full force, in the face,' he wrote in his dairy.

(For an account of McGonagall's unforgettable stage appearance as Macbeth, see the chapter on Theatre, p. 148.)

THE WORST AMERICAN POET

Julia Moore, 'the Sweet Singer of Michigan' (1847–1920), was so bad that Mark Twain said her first book gave him joy for 20 years.

Her verse is mainly concerned with violent death – the great fire of Chicago and the yellow fever epidemic proved natural subjects for her pen.

Whether the death was by drowning, by fits or by runaway sleigh, the formula was the same:

> Have you heard of the dreadful fate
> Of Mr P. P. Bliss and wife?
> Of their death I will relate,
> And also others lost their life
> (in the) Ashbula Bridge disaster,
> Where so many people died.

Even if you started out reasonably healthy in one of Julia's poems, the chances are that after a few stanzas you would be at the bottom of a river or struck by lightning. A critic of the day said she was 'worse than a Gatling gun' and in one slim volume counted 21 killed and 9 wounded.

Incredibly some newspapers were critical of her work, even suggesting that the sweet singer was 'semi-literate'. Her reply was forthright: 'The Editors that has spoken in this scandalous manner, have went beyond reason.' She added that 'literary work is very difficult to do'.

THE LEAST POETIC POET

Perhaps it was the result of a lifetime spent working as a Customs officer, but Edward Edwin Foot's poetry left nothing to chance or personal interpretation.

No sooner had he created an elusive poetic effect than

he introduced a footnote to explain it. For example in 'Disaster at Sea' he writes one to the very first line.

The captain scans the ruffled zone[1]

1. A figurative expression, intended by the Author to signify the horizon.

His greatest achievement was to write footnotes to the first two lines of his elegy on the death of Palmerston which were longer than the entire poem. These are the first two lines.

Altho' we[1] mourn for one now gone,
And he – that grey-hair'd Palmerston[2]

1. The nation.
2. The Right Honourable Henry John Temple, Viscount Palmerston, K.G., G.C.B., (the then Premier of the British Government) died at Brocket Hall, Herts. at a quarter to eleven o'clock in the forenoon of Wednesday, 18 October 1865 aged 81 years (all but two days), having been born on 20 October 1784. The above lines were written on the occasion of his death.

THE POET WHOSE BADNESS SAVED HIS LIFE

The most important poet in the seventeenth century was George Wither. Alexander Pope called him 'wretched Wither' and Dryden said of his verse that 'if they rhymed and rattled all was well'.

In our own time, *The Dictionary of National Biography* notes that his work 'is mainly remarkable for its mass, fluidity and flatness. It usually lacks any genuine literary quality and often sinks into imbecile doggerel'.

High praise, indeed, and it may tempt you to savour a typically rewarding stanza: It is taken from 'I loved a lass' and is concerned with the higher emotions.

She would me 'Honey' call,

> She'd – O she'd kiss me too.
> But now alas! She's left me
> Falero, lero, loo.

Among other details of his mistress which he chose to immortalize was her prudent choice of footwear.

> The fives did fit her shoe.

In 1639 the great poet's life was endangered after his capture by the Royalists during the English Civil War. When Sir John Denham, the Royalist poet, heard of Wither's imminent execution, he went to the King and begged that his life be spared. When asked his reason, Sir John replied, 'Because that so long as Wither lived, Denham would not be accounted the worst poet in England'.

THE MOST RIDICULOUS POET

The poetry of Margaret Cavendish, Duchess of Newcastle, received the ultimate accolade in 1667 when Samuel Pepys described it as 'the most ridiculous thing that ever was wrote'. Her method was to dictate in the middle of the night to servants specially posted on camp beds in the ante-room. Of particular interest to specialists like us is her poem 'What is liquid?'.

> All that doth flow we cannot liquid name
> Or else would fire and water be the same;
> But that is liquid which is moist and wet
> Fire that property can never get
> Then 'tis not cold that doth the fire put out.
> But 'tis the wet that makes it die, no doubt.

THE MOST UNSUCCESSFUL
VERSION OF THE BIBLE

The most exciting version of the Bible was printed in
1631 by Robert Barker and Martin Lucas, the King's
printers at London. It contained several mistakes, but one
was inspired – the word 'not' was omitted from the
Seventh Commandment and enjoined its readers, on the
highest authority, to commit adultery.

Fearing the popularity with which this might be
received in remote country districts, King Charles I
called all 1,000 copies back in and fined the printers
£3,000.

THE MOST REJECTED BOOK MANUSCRIPT

Mr Gilbert Young's book, 'World Government Crusade', has been rejected by more publishers than any other single manuscript. It has been sent back 105 times. 'A copy seems to come back every day,' he said. In 1973 he wrote to the Soviet Ambassador asking if a Russian publisher might be interested.

In 1958 this former insurance official founded the 'World Government and Old Age Pensioners Party'. He lost his deposit three times while contesting general elections at Bath, where he once held a political rally that attracted an audience of one.

The book is a distillation of all Mr Young's political views. His main policy is the establishment of one government for the whole world with one police force and one compulsory language. Another of his ideas is to turn Buckingham Palace into an old folks home.

THE SLOWEST SELLING BOOK

No author has ever equalled the record-breaking effort of David Wilkins whose translation of the New Testament from Coptic into Latin was published by the Oxford University Press in 1716.

When it went out of print in 1907 it had sold only 191 copies. This represents one copy every 139 days or about two and a half a year.

THE LEAST SUCCESSFUL AUTHOR

Mr William A. Gold of Australia became the all-time unsuccessful author when he earned 28 pence for writing more than three million words in an eighteen-year period of sustained creativity.

This remuneration came on 24 May 1974 for a contribution to a Canberra newspaper. He was 51 at the time.

His only other lapse had been sixteen years earlier when a 150-word book review was printed in the *Workers' Education Association Bulletin.* However this was done on the condition that he would not be paid for it.

THE LEAST PERCEPTIVE LITERARY CRITIC

The most important critic in our field of study is Lord Halifax. A most individual judge of poetry, he once invited Alexander Pope round to give a public reading of his latest poem.

Pope, the leading poet of his day, was greatly surprised when Lord Halifax stopped him four or five times and said, 'I beg your pardon, Mr Pope, but there is something in that passage that does not quite please me.'

Pope was rendered speechless, as this fine critic suggested sizeable and unwise emendations to his latest masterpiece. 'Be so good as to mark the place and consider at your leisure. I'm sure you can give it a better turn.'

After the reading, a good friend of Lord Halifax, a certain Dr Garth, took the stunned Pope to one side. 'There is no need to touch the lines,' he said. 'All you need do is to leave them just as they are, call on Lord

Halifax two or three months hence, thank him for his kind observation on those passages, and then read them to him as altered. I have known him much longer than you have, and will be answerable for the event.'

Pope took his advice, called on Lord Halifax and read the poem exactly as it was before. His unique critical faculties had lost none of their edge. 'Ay', he commented, 'now they are perfectly right. Nothing can be better.'

THE MOST OVERDUE LIBRARY BOOK

The most overdue book in the history of library services was a copy of Dr J. Currie's *Febrile Diseases*. It was taken out of the University of Cincinnati Medical Library in 1823 by Mr M. Dodd and returned on 7 December 1968 by his great-grandson.

In the intervening period it had accrued a fine estimated at 2,646 dollars (then £1,102).

THE LEAST SUCCESSFUL COLLECTOR

Betsy Baker played a central role in the history of collecting. She was employed as a servant in the house of John Warburton (1682–1759) who had amassed a fine collection of 58 first edition plays, including most of the works of Shakespeare.

One day Warburton returned home to find 55 of them charred beyond legibility. Betsy had either burned them or used them as pie bottoms. The remaining three folios are now in the British Museum.

The only comparable literary figure was the maid who in 1835 burned the manuscript of the first volume of Thomas Carlyle's 'The History of the French Revolution', thinking it was wastepaper.

'MAN FROM PORLOCK': A TRIBUTE

Few have had a more decisive influence on English literature than the outstanding 'Man From Porlock'.

In 1797 Samuel Taylor Coleridge took a cottage at Linton in Somerset to convalesce after illness. One day, under the influence of recuperative drugs, he fell asleep while reading about Kubla Khan's palace.

When he awoke, he found that he had composed in his dream a 300-line poem. Possessed with creative fervour, he sat down to write *Kubla Khan,* one of the great outpourings of the English language.

He had not got more than 54 lines down on paper when he was disturbed by a knocking on the door.

It was the seminal Man From Porlock who knew nothing about poetry and detained Coleridge for over an hour on some small matter of business – we know not what. By the time he left, the poet had completely forgotten his dream and the poem was never finished.

THE LEAST SUCCESSFUL EXHIBITION

The Royal Society for the Prevention of Accidents held an exhibition at Harrogate in 1968. The entire display fell down.

THE LEAST PERCEPTIVE ARTISTIC JUDGMENT

In the appreciation of modern art openmindedness is an essential quality. None have displayed it more than the hundred Frankfurt art lovers who accepted an invitation in spring 1978 to an exhibition of works by an 'exciting' new artist, Yamasaki – 'the discovery of the year'. The catalogue drew their attention to the 'convincing luminosity of his colours' and 'the excitement of his powerfully dynamic brushwork'. Within three hours all twenty-two exhibits had been bought for up to £500 each.

Excitement increased when the organiser, Mr Behrend Feddersen, announced that the artist would be making a guest appearance to answer questions about his work. How rewarding that the openmindedness of these art lovers was vindicated when a chimpanzee was brought in. 'I encouraged him to throw paint on 22 canvases,' said Mr Feddersen, and announced that the proceeds of the exhibition would be donated 'to the circus where he works.'

THE LEAST SUCCESSFUL DISPLAY OF A PAINTING

Between 17 October and 3 December 1961 Henri Matisse's painting *Le Bateau* was hung upside down in an art gallery without anyone noticing. It is estimated that 116,000 visitors to the New York Museum of Modern Art had passed through before this inversion was noticed by the artist's son. The painting showed a sailing boat and summer clouds with their reflections in the water.

THE WORST DRESSED
ROYAL SCULPTURES

In 1974 Mr J. Bulmer of Stocksfield, near Sunderland, was moved to create sculptures in clay, wood and papier-mâché of Queen Elizabeth II and her family.

However his pension did not run to the sort of garb in which Royalty is normally kitted out. Although art-lovers admired the way he had captured the Queen's expression, many were surprised to see that she was wearing what looked like an old maternity dress with leather arm patches. The Duke of Edinburgh had on trousers with an unusually low-slung crutch which hung somewhere just above his knees, while Princess Anne was wearing on her head something which could have started life as a lampshade. 'They look like tramps,' observed the leader of the Sunderland Council Conservatives.

THE LEAST SUCCESSFUL
FILM SCREENING

Probably the most unsuccessful film show was said to have occurred at the La Pampa cinema in Rio de Janeiro in November 1974.

During a screening of *The Exorcist* the audience was entirely distracted by a rat scampering to and fro before the screen. What little attention they were paying to the film was further diminished when an usherette appeared and pursued the rat with a mop.

Since this blocked the audience's view and entirely ruined a crucial vomiting scene of religious significance, the usherette was greeted with disgruntled cries of 'Get them off'.

Misconstruing the audience's wishes, she stunned the rat with her mop and proceeded to take all her clothes off. It was while dancing naked in the projector's light that she noticed the auditorium being cleared by armed police.

Explaining her behaviour, the usherette said afterwards, 'I thought the audience was calling for me. I was as surprised as anyone.'

BEST MISTAKES IN FILMS

In his *Filmgoer's Companion*, Mr Leslie Halliwell helpfully lists four of the cinema's greatest moments which you should get to see if at all possible.

In *Carmen Jones*, the camera tracks with Dorothy Dandridge down a street; and the entire film crew is reflected in the shop window.

In *The Wrong Box*, the roofs of Victorian London are emblazoned with television aerials.

In *Decameron Nights*, Louis Jourdain stands on the deck of his fourteenth century pirate ship; and a white lorry trundles down the hill in the background.

In *Viking Queen*, set in the times of Boadicea, a wrist watch is clearly visible on one of the leading characters.

THE LEAST SUCCESSFUL OPERATIC ARIA

Louis Quilico, a Canadian baritone, came close to perfecting the operatic art form in Chile in 1970 when he swallowed a pigeon's feather that wafted down from the roof.

The audience at a performance of *Rigoletto* watched with growing admiration as the feather circled haltingly from the rafters. As it approached, the singer threw back his head in song, swallowed the feather and fainted.

As if to show that bit-part players too have a vitally important role, the front of house manager had earlier rushed on stage to make an announcement. In his haste, he tripped over the soprano's dress and dived into the orchestra pit.

SIX

THE GLORY OF THE STAGE

The worst is not
So long as we can say, 'This is the
worst'.
King Lear

THE SHORTEST EVER WEST END RUN

THE WORST BOX OFFICE TAKINGS

THE WORST PLAYWRIGHT

THE WORST SHOW

THE WORST REVIEW

THE WORST EVER ACTOR

THE WORST SHAKESPEARE FESTIVAL

THE LEAST SUCCESSFUL PRODUCTIONS

THE WORST PROP

THE WORST EVER MEMBER OF
AN AUDIENCE

The best in this kind are but shadows
and the worst are no worse.
A Midsummer Night's Dream

THE WORST PLAYWRIGHT

This honour falls to Mr Edward Falconer. His interminable prose style reached astonishing new heights with the production on November 19, 1866 of *Oonagh, or, The Lovers of Lismona*. In it Falconer attempted to merge the stories of two quite separate novels, both fairly long in their original form.

The play started at 7.30 p.m. and went on, and on, and on. At 11 p.m., lulled by finest platitudes, the audience slumbered. Midnight came and the play meandered on its way. According to the critics, the 'audience folded their tents and stole silently away like Arabs', while the cast continued relentlessly onwards. By 2 a.m. only a handful of critics and Bohemians remained, slumped in bored slumber. With 3 a.m. looming the stage hands held a meeting and voted to take the law into their own hands. For the sake of everyone involved, they lowered the curtain. *Oonagh* was silenced. It did not have a second night.

THE MOST EMBARRASSED AUTHOR

Charles Lamb set a fine example on 10 December 1806 when he booed the premiere of his own play, 'Mr H'. Although he had packed the Drury Lane Theatre with his closest friends, they could not tolerate the work which purported to be a farce. Its sole humour centred upon the protagonist being called 'Hogsflesh' after a well-known cricketer. When 'the joke' came and went without laughter, a few gentle boos emanated from the stalls. These soon multiplied and from his seat in the front row, Lamb too gave way to hissing. The critic Crabb Robinson recollected that he 'was probably the loudest hisser in the house.'

Afterwards, Lamb said he agreed with the audience's verdict and started booing and hissing so they would not think he was the author. The management wanted to let the play run, but the playwright begged them to take it off.

THE SHORTEST EVER WEST END RUN

The shortest ever West End run was of a play called *The Lady of Lyons* by Lord Lytton. It opened on 26 December 1888, at the Shaftesbury Theatre. After waiting patiently for an hour, the audience was dismissed because no one could open the safety curtain.

THE WORST BOX OFFICE TAKINGS

The smallest amount of money ever taken at the box office during the run of a London play was £28.11s.0d. at the Opera Comique in the 1890s. This sum resulted from a four week run of a musical concerned with love in the desert, which was unscarred alike by memorable melodies and dialogue of note. In desperation the management advertised a free performance of this re-freshing musical comedy. Only five people attended and the show closed.

THE WORST SHOW

This was the 'Intimate Review' which opened and closed at the Duchess Theatre, London on March 11th 1930. When the curtain rose the stage was so cluttered that there was hardly any space for the actors. Each sketch had so much scenery that any set change took up to 20 minutes. The review was intimate, according to *The Times* critic, 'because we were always getting glimpses of things we were not meant to. Every time the curtains parted, squads of scene-shifters might be seen in action or in horrid precipitate flight.'

When this happened the first time, it was amusing; but when it happened every time a sketch started, audience hysteria set in. Each time the curtains opened, there were the scene shifters, as horrified as before. They looked up like terrified moles disturbed by torchlight and raced once more for the safety of the wings.

Then came Miss Florence McHugh's totally incomprehensible 'Hawaiian Idyll' in which, dressed as a dusky maiden, she paced the beach, hymning the pains of love. All would have been well except that, clearly visible through a transparent blue backdrop, two scene-shifting monsters were at war in the sea behind her.

At this rate the finale would have been on stage at about dawn, so the management moved straight to the final number. Six dancers, meant to represent Greek nymphs, lumbered hither and thither as best they could beneath the weight of monstrously large head-dresses. In one inspired manoeuvre two of the head-dresses became entangled, leaving Miss Florence McHugh, whose bravery was agreed upon by all the critics next morning, to sing the closing song, while other nymphs tried to untangle the unfortunate pair.

Next day the *Manchester Guardian* critic wrote: 'Spectators returned to their seats to be in at the death, to laugh with the conquered, not at them, and give a sporting cheer. Thumbs up or thumbs down? Who cares? Our good humour is restored. The show takes its final breath and, with a death rattle, expires. Enough!'

That afternoon the cast sent a brief statement to the *Evening Standard*: 'Everyone concerned was so much in agreement with the criticism of last night's performance that its closure was decided upon promptly. In regard to the accommodation on stage there was certainly an appearance of overcrowding.' They apologized to the audience, blamed lack of rehearsal and promised to re-open later in the year.

THE LEAST SUCCESSFUL PRODUCTIONS

In the closing years of the eighteenth century Mr George Frederick Cooke, the actor, became too drunk to play the principal role in Charles Macklin's 'Love a la Mode' at the Covent Garden Theatre. This made possible one of the few occasions when a play has been performed in public without its major character. After a brief discussion the cast decided to go on with the drama despite the absence of Sir Archy Macsarcasm, the play's main wit. During the performance the heroine, Charlotte, appeared more in need of an analyst than a suitor since she seemed to be in the permanent grip of an all-embracing hysteria. In one scene she was sitting alone on stage and had to say the following lines.

Charlotte: Ha ha ha.
Sir Archy: . . . .
Charlotte: I beg your pardon, sir, but – ha ha ha I am laughing – ha ha ha to think what – ha ha ha.
Sir Archy: . . . .

Charlotte: Ha ha ha! Pray how do you make that
             out?
Sir Archy: . . . .
Charlotte: Ha ha ha.

Act II contained a choice moment when the entire cast
laughed ('Omnes: Ha ha ha!') for no reason at all. It also
had Mordecai embracing thin air twice and Sir Callaghan
fighting the world's first unaccompanied duel. He was
interrupted in this venture, when Charlotte entered and
said: 'Oh bless me, what are you doing?'.

'ALAS, POOR HAMLET...
I KNEW HIM WELL...'

The same theatrical device was employed in 1787
when Hamlet was performed with no one playing its title
role. It was to have been played at the Richmond Theatre
by an inexperienced actor called Cubit who had pre-

viously been given only small walk-on parts. His debut as the Prince of Denmark had not been much relished by the first night audience. This so undermined Cubit's confidence that he was taken unwell on the second night just before curtain-up. With Hamlet ailing in his dressing room, the manager was obliged to request that the audience 'suffer a production' which omitted him entirely.

According to Sir Walter Scott the play was better received than on its first night, and many of the audience felt that it was an improvement on the complete play.

THE WORST REVIEW

The *Guinness Book of Records* mentions Alexander Woolcott's Broadway review of *Wham!* which read 'Ouch!' But there is one more dismissive. At the Duchess Theatre in London at the turn of the century there opened a show called *A Good Time*. Next morning it got the simple review, 'No'.

THE WORST EVER ACTOR

The worst actor ever to appear on a stage anywhere was Robert 'Romeo' Coates (1772–1842). Hardly ever did a production in which he figured end without riot.

His total incapacity to play any part whatever, combined with his insistence upon wearing diamonds from head to foot, regardless of role, and his tendency to 'improve' upon Shakespeare as he went along, made him immensely popular with astonished audiences up and down Britain.

His specialization was death scenes, which he used to preface by spreading a white silk handkerchief on the stage. These scenes were so protracted and so deliriously received that he frequently did encores, dying again.

Born in the West Indies, the son of a wealthy American sugar planter, he dabbled there in amateur dramatics.

When he inherited the estate at 35, Romeo Coates felt that he needed a larger platform and that he owed it to England to perform there. His belief in his own theatrical genius was unshakeable. Criticism he put down to envy.

He arrived in Bath in 1807 in a diamond-encrusted carriage, shaped like a seashell and emblazoned with a gilt cockerel bearing his appropriate family motto, 'While I live, I'll crow.' His habit of declaiming 'improved' passages of Shakespeare ('I fancy that is rather better') over breakfast at his inn soon brought him to the attention of the manager of the Theatre Royal.

While Coates awaited his British debut with pleasure, word got around as to the likely standard of his performance and all the tickets sold rapidly.

On that blustery November night he appeared in his greatest role –Romeo – a part which he was later forced to abandon because no actress would agree to play Juliet opposite him.

It started quietly enough, but when he entered the audience gave way to ecstatic cheers (which he stopped to acknowledge). Visually, Coates was always surprising and, on this occasion, he chose to dress his Romeo in a spangled sky-blue coat, bright crimson pantaloons and a white hat, excessively trimmed with feathers. Over all this was spattered a multitude of diamonds and the total effect ran quite counter to Shakespeare's description of the character as a 'quiet, virtuous and well-governed youth'.

The play continued in a hail of orange peel and whenever the audience crowed 'cock-a-doodle-do' at Coates he would break off, regardless of Juliet on the balcony, and crow back at them.

At one point the audience joined in a delighted chant of 'Off! Off! Off!' at which Coates, the gifted amateur, crossed his arms and stared at them with scorn and withering contempt.

That night the play got as far as the last act, but ended in riot when Coates suddenly re-entered with a crowbar, which was quite unnecessary and not mentioned in Shakespeare's text, to prize open the Capulet's tomb.

Of course, an actor of this calibre was soon in demand by London theatres and he arrived at the Haymarket Theatre on 9 December 1811. Here, playing Lothario in the first night of *The Fair Penitent,* Coates took longer to die on stage than anyone before or since. The audience sat politely, as his writhing figure was gripped by spasm after spasm, happy in the knowledge that it was only Act IV and that Coates would soon be dead, leaving a clear act to run without him. He died and the curtain fell.

After the interval, the gifted amateur came out before the curtain, dressed in regimental uniform, and announced that there would not be a fifth act that night. He would instead be reciting his favourite monologue.

After delighting London audiences for a further few years he retired from the stage due to bankruptcy.

THE WORST MACBETH

William McGonagall's first stage appearance was as Macbeth at Mr Giles's Theatre in Dundee. Realizing what a talent McGonagall had, Mr Giles said that he could only appear if a large sum of money was paid to the theatre in cash before the performance.

McGonagall said he considered this 'rather hard', but his fellow workers at the Seafield Handloom Works in Dundee had a whip round. They had heard him reciting Shakespeare at work, in his own unique way, and were keen to see him turned loose amidst professional actors.

'When the great night arrived,' McGonagall wrote in his diary, 'my shopmates were in high glee with the hope of getting a Shakespearian treat from me. And I can assure you, without boasting, they were not disappointed.'

When he appeared on stage, he was received with a perfect storm of applause. When he uttered his first line – 'So foul and fair a day I have not seen' – there was a deafening ovation.

The high spot came in the final scene, when Macduff is supposed to kill Macbeth in a sword fight. Unwisely, the actor playing Macduff told McGonagall to 'cut it short'.

Suspecting that the actor was jealous of the acclaim he was receiving, McGonagall refused to die. A new ending to 'Macbeth' seemed imminent.

'I continued the combat until he was fairly exhausted, and there was one old gentleman in the audience cried out: "Well done, McGonagall! Walk into him!" And so I did until he (Macduff) was in great rage, and stamped his foot, and cried out "Fool! why don't you fall?" And when I did fall, the cry was "McGonagall! McGonagall! Bring him out! Bring him out!" Until I had to come out and receive an ovation from the audience.'

THE WORST SHAKESPEARE FESTIVAL

If you want to hold a Shakespeare festival you could not improve upon the celebrations held at Stratford in 1769 to mark the bicentenary of Shakespeare's birth. They were organized by the actor, David Garrick.

For a start the festival was held five years late and in the wrong month. But it does not stop there. A torrential downpour flooded the fireworks and none of them lit. A wall collapsed in the Rotunda and stunned the main VIP, Lord Carlisle. Then the river burst its banks while Mrs Baddeley sang 'Soft thou gently flowing Avon' in a tent. The triumphal procession was called off twice and at the fancy dress ball revellers danced minuets up to their ankles in water. On the way out 150 of them fell into a ditch.

To top all that only one line of Shakespeare was spoken in the whole four days and that was misquoted.

'If there be any, speak,
for him have I offended.'

The bard actually wrote: 'If any, speak; for him have I offended.' On the last day the festival fizzled out and everyone went to the races to celebrate Shakespeare's birth there.

THE LEAST MOVING PAS DE DEUX

A performance of Kenneth MacMillan's ballet *Mayerling* on 19 October 1978 contained a *pas de deux* without equal. It was performed by an inspired pair, Miss Lynn Seymour and Mr David Wall.

The Covent Garden audience on Thursday 19 October

prepared their hankies as the tragic plot moved serenely towards the lovers' suicide pact.

In the final *pas de deux* Miss Seymour had hardly started when she tore her dress. Valiantly, Mr Wall attempted to rip off extraneous pieces which were trailing along the ground.

His well-meaning efforts, however, only caused the dress to divide into long streamers until the dancers struggled in a sudden mass of gauze bandages.

Since the dance involved writhing around in frenzied abandon, they looked like a stack of old rags possessed by the devil. Excitement grew as more and more of Miss Seymour was revealed. In the end she danced with the bandages instead of her partner.

The *Sunday Telegraph* ballet critic wrote of this fine performance: 'It was the first time I have watched Mayerling's suicide through a haze of tears, but what with trying to maintain a decent, sympathetic silence, and desperately struggling to control a rising hysteria, the ballet's marvels were for once quite lost on me.'

THE WORST PROP

The key man in the history of opera is not so much Richard Wagner as a clerk who worked with Richard Keene, a Wandsworth prop maker. In 1876 Wagner ordered a dragon to be made for the Bayreuth premiere of his opera 'Siegfried'. It was decided to send it over in sections. The tail arrived promptly, but then nothing was seen of the rest of the dragon for some weeks. Just as Wagner was losing all hope, a parcel arrived containing its torso. However, come the dress rehearsal, there was still no sign of the dragon's front end. At last the head came, but minus the neck.

For the first night the head had to be joined straight on to the body with the result that critics found the animal an endless source of merriment and Siegfried looked more like a bully than a hero. The neck never arrived. Two and half years later Wagner wrote: 'It is still lying lost in one of the stations between London and Bayreuth.' It was later said that the clerk had in error sent it not to Bayreuth in Germany, but to Beirut, capital of the Lebanon.

THE WORST MISHAP IN A STAGE PRODUCTION

There were historic scenes at the first and last night of 'Ecarte' at the Old Globe Theatre, London, in 1870. The play, written by theatre enthusiast Lord Newry, was laughed off the stage before the end.

Its failure was almost certainly due to a picnic scene early in the course of the play, for which Lord Newry, out of generosity and a concern for realism, provided hampers from Fortnum and Mason. These contained whole roast chickens, perigord pies, truffles and an un-limited supply of real champagne.

The cast drank freely and soon there was much joking amongst them which was quite inaudible to the audience. Then Miss Nita Nicotina the leading lady, forgot her words and, in an effort to recall them, gave a silly grin to the paying customers. Soon they were laughing, bump-ing into the props and leaning against scenery which would not support their weight. Then the (Australian) male lead, Mr Fairclough, started shouting all his lines and kept this up until he appeared to go to sleep.

'THEY MUST HAVE FUNNY
CAMELS IN GERMANY!'

In the next scene Nita appeared wearing one green and one red boot, whereupon the audience gave a yell of derisive laughter. This annoyed the actress who walked towards the footlights and said, 'What are you laughing at you beastly fools? When you have done making idiots of yourselves, I will go on with this (hiccup) beastly play.' This sealed the show's fate. The audience, now faced with a contingent of well-fed and cantankerous drunks, laughed and booed the play to a premature end.

THE SMALLEST EVER AUDIENCE

The smallest audience on record is two. They attended Mr W. H. C. Nation's pantomime 'Red Ridinghood' at Terry's Theatre in London at the turn of the century. The audience were both up in the gallery and they declined an offer to come down and sit in the stalls. As a result the cast did not see a single person throughout the show. What happened when they divided the audience in half to sing along with the villian and the hero can only be imagined.

THE WORST STAGE EFFECT

This unique moment of corporate nausea arose during the opening performance in 1945 of *The French Touch*, starring Arlene Francis and Brian Aherne.

Seeking to add novelty to this occasion, the play's highly inventive press agent had all the programmes and usherettes liberally doused in French perfume.

Had it stopped here these boudoir aromas might have proved an acceptable gimmick. However, the agent was so pleased with it that he arranged for perfume to be blown through the ventilating system as well.

The results were staggering. In no time at all half the audience had crawled out into the street and the other half was in deep sleep. The cast struggled queasily through to the end of the play.

THE WORST EVER MEMBER OF AN AUDIENCE

The highest accolade in this category must go to Mr Adam Drummond for his behaviour at the opening night of Oliver Goldsmith's 'She Stoops To Conquer' on Monday 15 March, 1773.

The manager of the Covent Garden Theatre had no confidence in the play. Only heavy pressure from Goldsmith's friends persuaded him to take the risk and stage it. This done, they had to ensure that it went well and took the unwise step of inviting Drummond who was known throughout London for his loud and infectious laugh. 'The neighing of a horse,' Goldsmith commented afterwards, 'was a whisper to it.'

However, the kindly Drummond forewarned them that they would have to tell him when to laugh, since he no more knew the right moment than did a cannon when to fire. He was planted in an upper box next to the stage. The plan was that when Dr Johnson in the front row laughed, someone would prod Drummond, setting off his infectious laugh and creating an air of general gaiety.

Well, Drummond laughed all right. Before long the attention of the spectators was so engrossed by his person that the play became a quite secondary object. Goldsmith's friends told Drummond that he might shut up now, but it was too late to rein the man in.

Whereas before he laughed on instruction, he now fancied that he found a joke in almost everything that was said. When Lumpkin and Miss Neville started fondling each other, he roared. When Miss Hardcastle spoke in a disguised voice, intended to be serious, he gasped for breath. As the fourth act opened to find Miss Neville and Hastings standing by the fire, he wiped tears from his eyes.

Eventually, he was turned around to face away from the stage, but still continued laughing at no one knows what.

SEVEN

WAR AND PEACE

Napoleon hoped that all the world
would fall beneath his sway.
He failed in this ambition, and
where is he today?
Anon. Lieutenant-Colonel, Poet

THE WORST GENERAL

THE FASTEST DEFEAT IN A WAR

THE WORST SPY

THE PEACE TREATY THAT WAS
TYPED BACK-TO-FRONT

THE LEAST SUCCESSFUL WARSHIP

THE LEAST SUCCESSFUL ATTEMPT TO
SHOOT DOWN ENEMY PLANES

THE WORST EVER DUEL

THE LEAST SUCCESSFUL
NAVAL REPAIRS

C'est magnifique, mais ce n'est pas la
guerre.

Marshall Bosquet

THE LEAST SUCCESSFUL AIR ATTACK

To celebrate 'Air Force Week' in 1975, thirty Peruvian fighter planes took part in a demonstration attack on fourteen old fishing boats.

These ramshackle old vessels were sailed out off the coast of Peru and abandoned as targets.

Then the impressive fighter force flew over the craft, high and low, strafing and bombing for the best part of fifteen minutes. To the amazement of the watching crowd, they failed to sink a single boat.

THE WORST GENERAL

Some men can steal victory from almost certain defeat. Major General Ambrose Everett Burnside usually progressed in exactly the opposite direction. No advantage, numerical or tactical, was so great that 'Burn', as he was affectionately known, could not throw it away in seconds.

During the American Civil War Burnside had 12,000 troops at his disposal. At the Battle of Antietam he overcame this advantage by ordering them to march in single file across an exposed bridge on which enemy guns were trained in large numbers. Only later did he learn that the river was only waist deep and could have been forded without danger at any point.

Two years later Burn planned to dynamite a trench along which his men could run in safety into the middle of the enemy camp. As the smoke was clearing his soldiers ran in only to find that they couldn't climb out again at the other end. The Confederate troops were more than surprised suddenly to find the whole enemy force trapped at their feet in a six foot pit. On hearing of this manoeuvre President Lincoln said: 'Only Burnside could have managed such a coup, wringing one last spectacular defeat from the jaws of victory.'

THE WORST TACTICIAN

During the Mexican-American War (1846–1848) General Antonio Lopez De Santa Anna lost every battle he fought, despite having modelled himself closely on Napoleon.

At the age of twenty he attended lectures on his hero and for some years adopted Napoleon's hairstyle, combing it from the back towards his forehead. In fact, he looked nothing whatever like Napoleon who was short and fat. Santa Anna was tall, skinny and had only one leg (he had lost the other in 1838 fighting the French and later held a special burial service for it at Santa Paula cemetery which was attended by a large number wishing to pay their respects).

Furthermore, he lacked almost all of Napoleon's strategic gifts. In one inspired 'surprise attack' he dressed all his troops in enemy uniforms. The chaos was indescribable and the plan a total failure.

During skirmishes with the Texans in the 1830s he was once taken prisoner by them, but, in a move of tactical brilliance, they released him. On 20 April 1836, showing the calmness of a great commander, he set up camp at the San Jacinto River overlooking a wood where Texans were known to be hiding and ordered his troops to take a siesta. At half past three in the afternoon his entire army was wiped out in only eighteen minutes. Santa Anna himself was enjoying a deep and refreshing sleep from which he was only roused by the continuing noise of marauding Texans. Realising that his entire army was being routed, Santa Anna didn't help matters by shouting 'The enemy is upon us' and leaving on a horse.

THE FASTEST DEFEAT IN A WAR

The fastest defeat in any war was suffered in 1896 by Said Khalid, the pretender Sultan of Zanzibar.

On 27 August the British battle fleet arrived to deliver an ultimatum. He declined to vacate the palace at the request of Rear Admiral Harry Holdsworth Rawson and so fighting broke out at 9.02 a.m. It reached its peak around 9.15 and was all over by 9.40.

The jewel of the Zanzibar defence force was its only warship, *The Glasgow*, an ageing ocean tramp. The turning point in the war came when it was sunk with only two shells.

The Sultan's palace was completely destroyed and, to add insult to total destruction, the British asked local residents to pay for the ammunition used in wrecking the place.

THE SOLDIERS WHO FOUGHT THE SECOND WORLD WAR FOR LONGEST

Lieutenant Hiroo Onoda of the Japanese army fought the Second World War until 3 p.m. on 10 March 1974, despite the continued absence of armed opposition in the later years. He used to come out of the jungle on his remote island in the Philippines and fire the odd bullet on behalf of Emperor Hirohito. In 1945 'come home' letters were dropped from the air but he ignored them believing it was just a Yankee trick to make him surrender. After he was found in 1974 it took six months to finally convince him that the war really was over.

But even after this surrender the Second World War still continued on the Island of Morotai where Private Teruo Nakamura maintained unbending resistance to the Allied Forces. This Indonesian island was finally liberated nine months later in December 1974.

THE COUNTRY WHICH FOUGHT TWO WORLD WARS SIMULTANEOUSLY

When drawing up the Versailles Peace Treaty at the end of the First World War, the great powers completely forgot about Andorra and failed to include it. Since the regular army of this tiny Pyrenean state comprised only one officer, six privates and four general staff, Andorra was perhaps the country least able to continue the First World War on its own.

It did not possess either artillery or machine guns, but, all soldiers wore on their uniforms buttons which read: 'Touch me if you dare,' the national motto.

Andorra's position worsened in 1939, when it found itself fighting two world wars simultaneously.

Finally on 25 September, it signed a private peace treaty with Germany officially concluding the First World War. This brought peace to Andorra for the first time in 44 years. Its current defence budget of £2 is spent entirely on blank ammunition for ceremonial purposes.

THE WORST SPY

Reversing the usual outcome of spying, Mr R. E. de Bruyeker gave the other side copious details about himself.

He broke into the NATO naval base at Agnano, near Naples, while spying on behalf of the Soviet Union in 1976 and removed a box of top secret documents.

He played his masterstroke, when he left his overnight bag behind in the office. It contained not only a hammer, a file, a bible and a copy of *Playboy*, but also full details about himself and his whereabouts. He was traced almost immediately.

THE PEACE TREATY THAT WAS
TYPED BACK-TO-FRONT

Sixty years after the First World War armistice was signed, the man who typed it admitted that much of it was back to front, but that nobody had noticed.

The significant person is Monsieur Henri Deledicq who was a clerk attached to the French HQ. On 7 November 1918 he was posted to the railway carriage at Rethondes in which the armistice was signed.

At the dictation of Marshall Foch he took down the form of words which would mean world peace. He then put some of the carbon papers in the wrong way round and whole chunks came out completely unreadable. 'It was 5 a.m. and I was too tired to notice', he said. Ten minutes later the armistice was signed by the war leaders, all of whom failed to notice the error.

Military clerk Deledicq was given a glass of port and then went on leave. It was not until some time later that Marshal Foch learned that the war ended in gibberish.

'He could hardly get over it' said Mr Deledicq who went on to become a wholesale wine merchant and to outlive everyone else present in that railway carriage.

THE LEAST SUCCESSFUL WARSHIP

In times of war self sacrifice is a paramount virtue. New heights were achieved in 1941 by HMS *Trinidad* when it fired a torpedo at a passing German destroyer. While sailing in the Arctic, its crew completely overlooked the effect of the icy water on oil in the torpedo's steering mechanism. The crew watched as it travelled at 40 knots towards its target and slowly became aware that the torpedo was starting to follow a curved course. In less than a minute it was pursuing a semi-circular route straight into the *Trinidad*'s path. Displaying the precision timing on which Naval warfare depends, the torpedo scored a direct hit on the ship's engine room and put HMS *Trinidad* out of action for the rest of the war.

THE GERMAN EFFICIENCY QUESTION

On 22 February 1940 a Luftwaffe bomber flying off the coast of Borkum, sighted two destroyers. In a sustained bout of Hunnish aggression, it strafed, bombed and cornered the vessels.

Rarely has one plane caused so much damage. The destroyers, the *Lebrecht Maass* and the *Max Schultz* both belonged to the German Navy.

THE LEAST SUCCESSFUL ATTEMPT TO SHOOT DOWN ENEMY PLANES

The high spot of the Royal Air Force activities during World War Two occurred at RAF Castle Bromwich in 1943. When airmen heard a plane landing late at night, they assumed it was one of many Spitfires tested there. Switching on an Aldis lamp, however, Aircraftman R. Morgan observed that it was a German bomber. As it taxied down the runway, he expressed the intention of having a crack at it with the Lewis gun and went off to get permission.

While the German plane revved its engines, Aircraftman Morgan tried to ring through to control. 'We had to crank like fury on the field telephone for permission to fire,' he said. By the time he got through the plane had taken off and was *en route* for Germany.

THE WEAPON THAT WAS TOO SECRET

The Franco-Prussian War is mainly notable for the introduction of the most secret weapon ever. The Mitrailleuse machine gun was the first of its kind and French officers confidently expected it to rout the enemy forces.

However, so great was the secrecy surrounding the new weapon that no instructions were issued as to how to work it until the first day of the war in 1870 by which time the men at the front had other things to occupy them.

THE WORST ARMS EXPERT

Nazi troops overran the armoury at Brest in 1940 and captured a new French secret weapon, the 15 inch 'Richelieu' gun. The delighted Germans immediately put an arms expert to work investigating this new weapon which, they believed, could swing the war their way if put to use quickly. However, our expert was not one to be rushed. Nothing if not thorough, he finally handed over a thick dossier, detailing every aspect of the gun's usage and capabilities in April 1944. Furthermore, he pointed out that it would be impossible to use the gun in the remaining 18 months of the war since during his four year investigation he had used up all the available ammunition in conducting his tests.

'..HOWEVER, MY FÜHRER, TESTS ON THE DOSSIER...'

THE LEAST SUCCESSFUL WEAPONS

The British contribution to this category was the No. 74 (ST) hand grenade, known affectionately in the Second World War as the 'sticky bomb'. A special feature was an adhesive coating which enabled it to stick to the side of an enemy tank. It also enabled it to stick to the thrower, which was generally what happened.

Once stuck, the soldier then had a considerate five-second delay in which to extricate himself. Even if he succeeded, only a practised shot putter could hope to lob the 4½ pound bomb far enough to ensure his own safety. It was the most unpopular weapon the British soldier has ever been asked to use and was soon discontinued.

For their part, the Japanese produced the Lunge Bomb, which comprised a long pole with a grenade and three spikes attached. To use it the infantryman approached the tank, rammed the spike through its side, and retired to a safe distance. However, since the safety pin had to be removed before this operation could begin, the ramming action almost invariably caused the bomb to detonate before the soldier had time to run away.

However, the prize for the most useless weapon of all time goes to the Russians, who, rather dourly, invented the dog mine. The plan here was to train the dogs to associate food with the underneath of tanks, in the hope that they would run hungrily beneath advancing Panzer divisions. Bombs were then strapped to their backs

'WELL, I SUPPOSE ITS BETTER THAN NOTHING...'

which endangered the dogs to a point where no insurance company would look at them.

Unfortunately, they associated food solely with Russian tanks and forced an entire Soviet division into retreat. The plan was abandoned on day two of the Russian involvement in World War Two.

THE LEAST SUCCESSFUL
TARGET PRACTICE

As part of a training exercise off Portsmouth in 1947, the destroyer, HMS *Saintes*, was required to fire at a target pulled across its bows by the tug *Buccaneer*.

It fired a shell, missed the target and sank the tug.

THE MOST UNSUCCESSFUL
NINE-GUN SALUTE

Rounding Cape Horn, the yacht *Adventure*, entered by the Royal Navy for the 1974 Round the World race was given a nine-gun salute of welcome by HMS *Endurance*, a 3,600 ton ice breaker.

Part of the sixth shot hit the 55 foot yacht, *Adventure*, and wrecked its headsails. The ten-man crew, which had just won the previous leg of the race, had to spend the rest of the day sewing them up.

THE UGLIEST BUILDING EVER CONSTRUCTED

In 1955 the British Ministry of Defence erected a reinforced concrete blockhouse in Scotland which was so ugly that planting a forest round it was later made a condition of sale.

In 1975 the Ministry told Lord Cawdor, on whose land it was built, that the Army had no further use for it. He then had the problem of how to sell a single storey grey concrete blockhouse, 175 feet long by 85 feet wide, with no windows, a box design, one camouflaged door and a flat roof.

In a newspaper advertisement he said, 'For sale: Reinforced concrete eyesore. Would suit nervous spy or mushroom farmer with dangerous wife for whom outhouse with five foot walls ideal. Offers and suggestions, however inane, invited for monument to corrupted endeavour. Forest planting a condition of sale.'

THE LEAST SUCCESSFUL NAVAL REPAIRS

In September 1978 a paint scraper worth 30 pence was accidentally dropped into a torpedo launcher of the US nuclear submarine *Swordfish* and jammed the loading piston in its cylinder. For a week divers tried to free the piston while *Swordfish* was waterborne but all attempts failed. She had to be dry-docked and subsequent repairs cost 171,000 dollars (£84,000).

THE WORST EVER DUEL

For many years the duel fought between Sir Hierome Sankey and Sir William Petty in 1645 was without equal. The dispute arose in London over a matter of honour now lost in the mists of time.

Sir Hierome was a tough character and Sir William, being of a nervous disposition, was reluctant to fight him.

Since Sir Hierome had initiated the duel, Sir William had the choice of venue and weapons. Brilliantly, he chose a pitch-dark cellar and two carpenters' axes which neither of them could lift.

This stood as the worst until December 1971, when the duel between a Uruguayan Field Marshall and a fellow General quite surpassed it. This occurred when the Field Marshall called his colleague 'a socialist'. They decided to settle the matter honourably.

Meeting at dawn in one of Montevideo's public parks, the two soldiers fired 37 rounds at each other from a distance of 25 paces. Neither man was hurt.

Explaining this surprisingly high level of inaccuracy, the Field Marshal's second said they had failed to put on their glasses before commencing their back-to-back walk.

THE LEAST SUCCESSFUL
MANOEUVRE

New standards for reversing into a jetty were set on 17 May 1966 by the Royal Navy frigate *HMS Ulster*. During training exercises in the Tamar Estuary at Plymouth its starboard engine control became stuck in the 'half astern' position. Attempts to free it only jammed the handle on 'full astern'. The engine room obeyed the orders and soon the ship was gathering speed and sailing backwards straight for a stone jetty. The captain telephoned the engine-room, but there was no reply. He then ordered both the anchors to be dropped in an attempt to slow the ship down and sent his officer of the watch down to the engine room to tell them what was happening. On the way there he met the entire ship's company all going in the opposite direction to emergency stations. He was unable to make any headway.

The frigate eventually hit the jetty travelling at 8 knots. The impact shortened the ship by seven feet and compressed the air inside it. This caused the only casualty. A sailor who was half way through a hatch at the moment of impact was shot 15 feet into the air and landed safely on the jetty.

EIGHT

THE BUSINESS OF POLITICS

Politics is a field where the choice
lies constantly between two blunders.
John Morley MP, February 1887

THE WORST POLITICIAN

THE WORST ORATOR

THE WORST SPEECH WRITER

THE INTERPRETER WHO GOT IT WRONG

THE LEAST SUCCESSFUL UNVEILING

THE WORST MAYOR

THE WORST HIJACKERS

THE LEAST SUCCESSFUL COUP

THE LEAST SUCCESSFUL
REVOLUTIONARIES

Well, thank God, at last we have got
a ministry without one of those men of
genius in it.

*A Peer, commenting on Lord Addington's
newly-formed Government*

THE WORST MAYOR

From our point of view the most important mayor ever to hold office was Señor José Ramon Del Cuet.

In June 1978 he resigned as Mayor of Coacaloco in Mexico, feeling that his record in office was poor. This selfless decision was reached with the help of 4,000 local voters who stormed the town hall, seized the mayor and forced him to eat 12 lb. of bananas before signing his resignation.

THE ELECTION THAT HAS PROVOKED LEAST INTEREST

Mr George Kindness was elected to Machars Community Council in the Aberdeen district by the only vote cast in the whole election.

After the 1973 result was announced, Councillor Kindness assured reporters that he had not voted for himself. 'I didn't bother,' he said, while posing for victory photographs in a tee-shirt.

His rivals did not demand a recount.

A SPECTACULAR FAILURE OF DEMOCRACY

In 1928 Charles King was elected President of Liberia by a majority of 600,000. This would be remarkable enough in any election, but as Graham Greene reports in his book

Journey without Maps, there were only 15,000 registered voters. While I was trying to get more information on this, a man at the Liberian Embassy expressed 'extreme surprise' that anyone would find this election different from any other in Liberia.

THE WORST POLITICIAN

Only eight politicians have been awarded the ultimate accolade by the British electorate. The pioneer was Lord Garvagh. When standing as Liberal candidate for Reigate in 1832, he evoked such widespread indifference that he became the first person to poll no votes at all in a general election.

The excitement was intense. It was not until seven years later that Mr L. Oliphant (Liberal) was able to repeat the achievement.

In 1841 two Chartists, Mr W. Thomason and Mr W. Edwards, did it at Paisley and Monmouth respectively. Six years later a third Chartist, Mr G. T. Harney, repeated the triumph at Tiverton and before long the Chartist Party was out of business altogether.

The Conservative Party are, by definition, slow to adopt new trends and it was not until 1847 that Viscount Lascelles threw caution to the wind. He made the break through at Tewkesbury where it proved so popular that Mr H. Brown repeated the feat on behalf of the Liberal Party in 1859.

The last person to achieve nought was Mr F. R. Lees at the 1860 Rippon by-election. The art has now been completely lost since candidates are now allowed to vote for themselves.

THE WORST ORATOR

No man ever debated regularly in the British Parliament with such an entire want of the conventional public speaking abilities as the magnificent Lord Castlereagh (1769–1822).

He rose to a level of exalted badness which few could hope to emulate. His main gift was that he could speak fluently for an hour without his meaning once becoming apparent to listeners.

He was so inspiring that MPs passed the time collecting the worst of his rhetoric. In this way posterity has been able to savour the lingering magnificence of such phrases as:

'Men turning their backs upon themselves' and

'The constitutional principle wound up in the bowels of the monarchical principle.'

George Henry Jennings, a Parliamentary historian, said that Castlereagh's rhetoric 'often baffled alike the gravity of the Treasury bench and the art of the reporter, and left the wondering audience at a loss to conjecture how anyone could ever exist, endowed with humbler pretensions to the name of orator.'

THE WORST SPEECH WRITER

Warren Gamaliel Harding wrote his own speeches while president of the USA in the 1920s and people queued up to pay tribute.

H. L. Mencken said: 'He writes the worst English that I have ever encountered. It is so bad that a sort of grandeur creeps into it.'

When Harding died, E. E. Cummings said: 'The only man, woman or child who wrote a simple declarative sentence with seven grammatical errors is dead.'

Here is a rewarding sample of the man's style: 'I would like the government to do all it can to mitigate, then, in understanding, in mutuality of interest, in concern for the common good, our tasks will be solved.'

THE MP WHO LOST A MOTION DESPITE EVERYONE AGREEING WITH HIM

Henry Grattan (1750–1820) was utterly incapable of writing the simplest thing quickly. When called upon to scrawl down any brief sentence, he invariably failed to do it within the allotted time. A short note to a constituent could take anything up to an hour and dozens of rewrites.

As a result of this magnificent defect, he once managed to lose a motion in the Irish House of Commons, despite everyone supporting it.

Grattan spoke readily enough on his theme and the house clearly shared his views. The Speaker asked him to word a formal motion so they might vote formally upon it.

Four lines would have embraced it and 30 seconds seen the job through. But Grattan was more thorough. He wrote and tore, and wrote and tore. Then he wrote and scratched his head and tore. Then he rubbed his brow and wrote nothing. Once, he wrote and wrote and wrote and then tore. Eventually, the house lost all patience and a member proposed that instead of a formal resolution, the minister should give a verbal pledge. To this Grattan agreed, but the rest of the house objected. The motion was lost.

THE LEAST SUCCESSFUL LORDS

Richard Coke, the fifth Earl of Leicester was a member of the House of Lords for 22 years before making his only speech. In so doing he ended an illustrious family record for silence. His father did not speak in 32 years of membership nor his grandfather in 67. This meant that no Coke spoke for 120 years.

The third Earl once shouted 'jolly good' during somebody else's speech, but then you have to wait until the early 1960s for anything comparable (the fifth Earl said he would like to speak on capital punishment, but then changed his mind).

Richard Coke explained that they were all too busy running a sub-post office at their stately home, Holkham Hall in Norfolk, which the first Earl had opened in 1834.

Then, in January 1972, the fifth Earl decided that he would 'rather like to take the plunge'. He started with a joke. 'This is not a case of too many Cokes spoiling the broth,' he said.

He went on to say that pollution was a bad thing and that untested artificial fertilizers were ruining the countryside.

'It took a lot out of me,' said the Earl whose family motto is 'He is prudent who is patient.'

THE INTERPRETER WHO GOT IT WRONG

A leading figure in this field is Mr S. Seymour who translated into Polish the speeches of President Carter during his 1977 tour of Poland.

His inspired translation of the address at Warsaw Airport was touched with genius. When President Carter spoke of his 'desires for the future,' Mr Seymour stylishly rendered this into Polish as his 'lusts for the future.'

He reached new heights of mastery, when translating

an innocent comment about the flight from Washington that morning.

Instead of the dull platitude actually spoken, the astonished Poles understood President Carter to have said that he had 'left America never to return.'

Mr Gierek, the Polish leader, said, 'I had to grit my teeth from time to time. But one must not be rude to ladies or interpreters.'

THE LEAST SUCCESSFUL UNVEILING

The Prime Minister set a very high standard in 1978. At a reception held to open the new Anglo-Austrian Society premises in Queen Anne's Gate, London, Mr James Callaghan was required to unveil a wooden plaque.

'Why don't you tell me when you'd like me to pull the ribbon?' the Prime Minister asked the hordes of photographers crowding round him.

'I tell you what,' he said genially, 'I'll count to five and then I'll pull it.'

This he duly did and on the count of five, lights flashed and cameras clicked, as he pulled the entire plaque bodily from the wall.

THE POLITICIAN WHO DID NOT HAVE A MOTION SECONDED IN HIS ENTIRE CAREER

In 16 years on Huddersfield Council, Alderman William Wheatley never had a motion seconded.

Between 1905 and 1921 this excellent man, a member of the Labour Party, regularly put motions before the council on a wide range of topics. Not once in that period was any member of the council sufficiently keen on his suggestion to vote that it even be discussed.

A Wheatley relative said, 'In our family we have a saying, "You're as useless as Uncle William." '

THE MOST FAILED ASSASSINATION ATTEMPTS ON A POLITICAL LEADER

By 1974 an estimated twenty-four attempts had been made on Fidel Castro's life by political enemies. By 1978 the perhaps inflated estimate of sixty was mentioned by Castro himself.

One plot failed because two poison capsules dissolved while hidden in a pot of cold cream. Another came unstuck because the brunette agent sent to finish Castro off turned out to be in love with him and more likely to cook him a TV supper than kill him.

Badly aimed poison pellets did more damage to Cuban trees than Dutch Elm disease ever could and, according to one story, an array of exploding seashells missed Castro by forty minutes but fused all the traffic lights in downtown Havana.

Three assassins were arrested carrying a bazooka

across a university campus and another put a poisoned chocolate milkshake in the freezer compartment by mistake. By the time anyone offered it to Castro, it had gone solid and was impossible to drink.

THE WORST HIJACKERS

We shall never know the identity of the man who in 1976 made the most unsuccessful hijack attempt ever. On a flight across America, he rose from his seat, drew a gun and took the stewardess hostage.

'Take me to Detroit,' he said.

'We're already going to Detroit,' she replied.

'Oh . . . good,' he said, and sat down again.

Few other cases come anywhere near this. In 1967 a drunk Arab hijacked a plane and demanded that he be taken to Jerusalem. For his own safety, the crew explained there was a war on there and, being an Arab, he would probably get shot on sight. 'He was so drunk he had to be protected,' the captain said afterwards.

THE LEAST SUCCESSFUL COUP

In 1964 a fascist coup was organized in Rome. Gathering on the outskirts of the city, the right wingers planned a stampede to the centre prior to overthrowing the government.

However, the majority were not from Rome itself and so the bulk of the stampede got lost in the back streets.

Five years after the coup, the authorities discovered that it had taken place and set up a commission to investigate it.

In 1974 a second coup was called off in Calabria due to torrential rain. 'It was coming down in buckets,' said the commandant in charge.

THE LEAST SUCCESSFUL REVOLUTIONARIES

As Woody Allen observed in his 'Brief yet helpful guide to civil disobedience'; 'In perpetrating a revolution there are two requirements. Someone or something to revolt against and someone to actually show up and do the revolting.' Almost perfect in this last category was the Easter Uprising of 1916. Of the 12,000 members of the Irish Volunteer Force due to arrive on Sunday 23 April, only 1,500 arrived on the right day. The remaining 10,500 revolutionaries had been so confused by the plethora of constantly changing orders that they did not rise up until the following day.

Addressing those who did arrive, the leader, Patrick Pearse, read out the Proclamation of the Republic and ordered that copies of it be posted up throughout Dublin. He then discovered that the military council had forgotten to buy any glue. As a result the first looting occurred – a packet of flour was seized from a grocer's shop to make an adhesive paste.

THE LEAST SUCCESSFUL
NATIONAL MOURNING

India was swept with grief on 22 March 1979 when the Indian Prime Minister, Mr Morarji Desai, informed Parliament that Jayaprakash Narayan, the patriot and elder statesman, had died in a Bombay hospital.

The Prime Miniser delivered a moving eulogy and Parliament was adjourned. Flags were lowered to half mast. The news was flashed all over the sub-continent. Funeral music was broadcast on All-India Radio. Schools and shops closed down throughout the land. The entire nation plunged into mourning for over an hour.

Everyone was shaken by the news, none more so than Mr Jayaprakash Narayan who was in bed convalescing.

'I'm sorry about that', said the Prime Minister afterwards. The information had apparently come from the director of the Intelligence Bureau, one of whose staff had seen a body being carried out of the hospital.

NINE

LOVE AND MARRIAGE

A man who cannot make mistakes
cannot do anything.
Bernard's Bingo Magazine

THE LEAST SUCCESSFUL LATIN LOVER

THE LEAST SUCCESSFUL DATE

THE LEAST SUCCESSFUL EMBRACE

THE MOST UNSUCCESSFUL ATTEMPT
TO DIE FOR LOVE

THE LEAST SUCCESSFUL ABDUCTION

THE MOST CHAOTIC WEDDING
CEREMONY

THE LEAST WHIRLWIND ROMANCE

THE LEAST FAITHFUL HUSBAND

THE MOST DIVORCES FROM
THE SAME PERSON

THE LEAST SUCCESSFUL ALIBI

If anything can go wrong it will.
Murphy's Law

THE LEAST WHIRLWIND ROMANCE

In 1900 Octavio Guillen met the girl who would one day be his wife. Two years later he announced his engagement to Adriana Martines and everyone said they made a lovely couple.

They still made a lovely couple in 1969, when they cast caution to the wind and got married in Mexico City. They were both 82 and had been engaged for 67 years.

THE LEAST SUCCESSFUL LATIN LOVER

In 1977 Signor Paco Vila, a student from Palermo in Italy, was carried out on a stretcher, after having his cheek caressed in a discotheque.

In many respects Signor Vila had the mainstream Latin interests and approach. 'I am mad about big English women,' he said, after regaining consciousness in a hospital bed. 'But they scorn me because I lack the weight.'

He was on the skinny side and in a valiant effort to offset this, he started wearing thick woolly jumpers beneath his shirt.

At this particular discotheque he had so disguised his problem that he succeeded in getting an English girl on holiday at Palmero to dance with him.

During one of his more frisky rumbas, he used so much energy that, when the girl boldly stroked his cheek, he collapsed in a dead faint. When examined later by doctors, he was found to be wearing 17 woolly sweaters under his shirt and to weigh only seven stones.

THE BURGLAR WHO FELL IN LOVE WITH HIS VICTIM

One of the great romantic encounters occurred in November 1978 between a Streatham burglar and a blonde lady into whose house he had broken.

As soon as he saw the lady he changed his tack entirely, choosing this, of all unlikely moments, to woo her.

After thirty minutes he was getting on so famously that he tried to kiss her. To his horror, she not only refused, but also felled him with a right-hand punch, a left-hand jab and a half-nelson.

In this state she frogmarched him to the porter's lodge, while hitting him on the head with a spare shoe.

'She was no ordinary helpless female,' the burglar commented, on discovering that prior to a sex change she had been employed as a bricklayer.

THE LEAST SUCCESSFUL DATE

In the spring of 1978 Mr Tom Horsley, a 30-year-old accountant from San José, invited Miss Alyn Chesselet out for the evening. At the very last minute, she cancelled.

Mr Horsley then sued her.

He went to the San Francisco Small Claims Court and filed a suit against Miss Chesselet on the grounds that she had 'broken an oral contract to have dinner and see the musical *The Wiz*'.

Mr Horsley, who made a 100-mile round trip to visit her, informed the court that he wanted to be paid for two hours of driving to and from San Francisco at his minimum rate of £4.70 an hour as a certified public accountant, and 9.4 pence a mile in car expenses. His claim was for £18.80 plus a £1.10 filing fee and a £1.10 to serve court papers – a total of £21.

When the court notified Miss Chesselet, a 30-year-old waitress at the Vasuvio Cafe in San Francisco, she said that Mr Horsley was 'nuts'.

THE LEAST SUCCESSFUL EMBRACE

In 1976 Dr Brian Richards of Deal in Kent discovered one of the great love stories of all time, while in Regent's Park, London.

He came across a semi-clad gentleman who had slipped a disc while enjoying himself in the back of a sports car with his girl-friend.

Since the man was transfixed with agony, his girl-friend was unable to get out for help. In desperation she jammed her foot against the hooter button.

This attracted Dr Richards, an ambulanceman, a fire-man and a large crowd of passers-by who formed a circle around the car. 'You'll never get them out of there,' said the fireman who then set about cutting the back off the car.

Trained for desperate situations, two women volun-tary workers arrived and began serving hot sweet tea through the window. 'It was like the blitz,' one of them commented.

Eventually, the lover was carried off in agony. Ambulancemen told the girl-friend that his recovery prospects were good. 'Sod him,' she replied. 'What's worrying me is how I shall explain to my husband what's happened to his car.'

THE LEAST SUCCESSFUL PORNOGRAPHIC BOOKSELLER

In February 1970 a Swiss pornographic bookseller was fined the equivalent of £47 and given a ten-month suspended sentence because his books were not sufficiently pornographic.

Angry residents of Biel took him to court because his wares were not as 'sexually erotic' as his advertising campaign had led them to believe. At the hearing many of them expressed the view that had they been interested in veils, curtains, cushions and household plants they would have bought a furnishing catalogue.

THE MOST UNSUCCESSFUL ATTEMPT TO DIE FOR LOVE

When his fiancée broke off their engagement in 1978, Senor Abel Ruiz of Madrid decided to kill himself for love. Reviewing the possibilities available on such occasions, he opted to prostrate himself before the Gerona to Madrid express. However, jumping in its path he landed between the rails and watched the train pass safely over him. He suffered only minor injuries and promptly received first aid at Gerona Hospital.

Later that day Ruiz tried again. This time he jumped in front of a passing lorry, but only acquired some more bruises. His rapid return to the hospital led doctors to call a priest who made Mr Ruiz see the folly of his acts. Eventually he decided to carry on living and look for a new girlfriend. Glad to be alive, he left the hospital and was knocked down by a runaway horse. He was taken back to Gerona Hospital for the third time that day, seriously injured this time.

THE LEAST SUCCESSFUL ABDUCTION

In August 1972 Mr Darsun Yilmaz of Damali on the Black Sea was spurned by his neighbour's daughter and decided to abduct her. Soon after midnight the intrepid Yilmaz arrived in his beloved's garden with a ladder. Once in her room, he threw a blanket over her head and carried her down to the car, whispering torrid endearments into that end of the blanket where one might reasonably expect her ear to be.

Away they sped into the night, joy in his heart and stars in the sky. However, when he unwrapped his precious cargo and pursed his lips for a kiss he discovered to his astonishment that it was the girl's 91-year-old granny, who took this welcome opportunity to beat him up.

THE SHORTEST PERIOD OF MARITAL BLISS

Jerzy and Kathryn Sluckin got married at Kensington register office in November 1975. Within an hour of the wedding Kathryn surprised her husband and relatives when she announced at the reception, 'It won't work' and vanished. Her husband later heard that his wife was living in a Divine Light Meditation Commune in Finchley.

'I had a few doubts before the wedding,' she admitted afterwards, 'but didn't want to say anything.'

THE BRIDES WHO MARRIED THE WRONG GROOMS

At a Moslem double wedding in Jeddah, a Saudi Arabian gentleman gave his two veiled daughters away to the wrong grooms. During the ceremony in December 1978 he accomplished a slip of the tongue when he announced his approval of the marriages to the ma'zoun (the registrar) and confused the names of the brides and grooms. A few days after the wedding the girls told their father that divorce would be unnecessary since they were quite satisfied with their husbands.

While I was trying to get more details a Saudi journalist explained: 'This is happening all the time.'

THE LEAST FAITHFUL HUSBAND

Fredrick Augustus was Elector of Saxony and later King of Poland. When he died in 1699, his household records revealed that he had produced only one child in wedlock. It was called Maurice. However the records also showed that Augustus' marital devotion occasionally faltered. He was also responsible for 345 illegitimate children.

THE MOST CHAOTIC WEDDING CEREMONY

It would be difficult to organize a wedding which ran less smoothly than the one held in July 1973 at Kingston in Surrey.

For a start the vicar went sick and they had to rustle up a pastoral replacement to seal the knot at short notice. Matters worsened considerably when the groom put the ring on his bride's finger and she had a blackout. She remained unconscious for 20 minutes.

While she was carried off and revived, the choir sang 'Jesu, Joy of man's desiring' to disguise a welter of fanning, slapping, and blowing.

Once the bride had regained consciousness the ceremony was completed. The happy couple made their way down the aisle. In a shower of nuts and confetti, they approached the going-away car which was now seen to contain a cement mixer. The groom took this opportunity to tell guests that the honeymoon hotel had burnt down and instead, they were going to spend the time building a septic tank.

Strangely modest, the couple have asked to remain unnamed.

THE MAN WHO WAS DIVORCED TWICE IN FIFTEEN MINUTES

Mr Alhaji Mohamed, a security officer from Walworth, was divorced by two wives inside a quarter of an hour on 17 July 1975 at the High Court in London. The presiding Judge, Sir George Baker, said, 'This must be the very first time in these courts that two ladies have been able to divorce the same gentleman in one afternoon.'

Under Muslim law Mr Mohamed, is entitled to four wives. The first decree went to Mrs Adiza Mohamed who had lived apart from her husband for two years. Minutes later, the second was granted to Mrs Rabi Mohamed who wanted to marry someone else.

THE WORLD DIVORCE RECORD HOLDER

In December 1978 seventy-one year old Glynn de Moss Wolfe made plans to marry for the twenty-second time. 'This could be true love at long last,' he said.

A one-time marriage counsellor, he claims that he can remember all his wives. 'Helen was the first in 1931. Then came Marjorie, Margie, Mildred and Adele in quick succession. In 1943 I married Mary, but her father wanted to kill me and that put a damper on everything. Then there was Mary A., Peggy Lou, Beverly, Shirley, Sherri – twice, Kathy, Paulette, Didi, Bobbie, Demerle, Esther, Gloria, Maria, Lupitia and now Eva.'

'Divorce doesn't upset me,' he said, 'It's another racoon skin on the wall.'

THE MOST DIVORCES FROM
THE SAME PERSON

In January 1970 Dorothy and David King Funk obtained their fifth divorce from one another.

The complaint for divorce in this last case was filed by Mrs Funk, seven months after their fifth wedding ceremony.

The couple first married in December 1950 and this lasted seven years. They were also divorced in 1962, 1964 and 1965. On each occasion the marriage was ruled to have broken down irreparably.

THE LEAST SUCCESSFUL ALIBI

During his divorce hearing in July 1978, a London window cleaner was asked to explain what he and 'the other woman' were doing in his bedroom with the lights out. He replied: 'Playing snooker.'

The judge, Aubrey Myerson Q.C., said: 'To my mind it is rather difficult to play a game of snooker in a room where the lights are off.'

Mr Charlton was next asked to explain the noises of passionate abandon which his wife heard coming from the house. He replied that it was 'an expression of surprise or disappointment made when playing a difficult shot.'

He was then asked why, on another occasion, the 'other woman' had been seen undressed from the waist down. Mr Charlton's explanation was that she 'was doing some sewing and altering her slacks.'

His wife did not believe it and nor did the judge.

TEN

STORIES WE FAILED TO PIN DOWN

It was I myself who personally and
accidentally goofed.
David Ogilvy

THE WORST ATTEMPTS AT CAR REPAIRS

THE MOST UNSUCCESSFUL HUMAN
CANNON-BALL

THE LEAST SUCCESSFUL ELECTION

THE LEAST SUCCESSFUL COMPLAINT

THE LEAST SUCCESSFUL POLICE
STATEMENT

THE WORST FOX HUNT

THE LEAST SUCCESSFUL CHORAL
CONTEST

THE LEAST SUCCESSFUL AUDIENCE
PARTICIPATION

THE MOST UNSUCCESSFUL ATTEMPT
TO PROPOSE MARRIAGE

THE LEAST SUCCESSFUL
HOUSEPARTY HOLIDAY

The history of mankind is an immense sea of errors in which a few obscure truths may here and there be found.

C. Debaccaria

There comes a point when we all have a clear duty to give up. I reached that point while trying to pin down the following stories, all of which eluded research and verification.

THE MOST UNSUCCESSFUL CANNON-BALL

On two occasions Miss 'Rita Thunderbird' has remained inside the cannon despite gunpowder encouragement to do otherwise.

She performs in a gold lamé bikini and on one of these occasions (at Battersea in 1977), Miss Thunderbird remained lodged in the cannon, while her bra was shot across the River Thames.

THE WORST ATTEMPTS AT CAR REPAIRS

In 1976 a travelling salesman had bought a new car and for fully 24 hours its performance had been perfect in every respect. However, by the following day, all its forward gears had jammed.

'I was too busy at the time to get it fixed,' he said. As the reverse gear was still in good order, our man decided that thereafter he would drive everywhere backwards. 'I have covered 80,000 miles since then.'

THE WORST FLEET

In the early 1970s a fleet of US Navy tankers blazed a trail through naval history adorned with classic mishaps. On one occasion one of them had to sail from Britain to the Caribbean backwards, because its engines got jammed in reverse. A sister ship became known as the 'Pink Panther' after the normal red and grey paint used on it had been accidentally mixed. And a third tanker went full speed into Los Angeles harbour and damaged a freighter so badly that it had to be towed away for scrap.

THE LEAST SUCCESSFUL ELECTION

The worst ever election was held in June 1974 when the voters of a town in Western Australia re-elected as mayor the man whose death had caused the election in the first place.

Apologizing to the 8,731 electors who had voted to have the late mayor reinstated for a further year, the town clerk apparently described the occurrence as 'a bad mistake.'

It was, he said the result of confusion on the part of those preparing the ballot sheet.

When it was announced that the mayor had been re-elected by a sizeable majority, there was, not surprisingly, a considerable public outcry. A goodly part of it came from the sister-in-law of the deceased.

On hearing the result, she is alleged to have said, 'I know George was very popular with the townsfolk, but I was still surprised to hear his election victory announced on the radio, driving back from the crematorium.'

THE LEAST SUCCESSFUL COMPLAINT

In 1975 a thief stole a radio from a shop in Ashton-under-Lyme. When he got home and turned it on, he found that it was defective.

He then went back and demanded that it was repaired free of charge. Unable to produce a receipt, his request was turned down, so he went round to the police station and complained.

During his interview with the duty sergeant he was charged with theft.

THE LEAST SUCCESSFUL POLICE STATEMENT

In 1978 a man charged with murder escaped from the custody of the Irish police. The Garda Press Office, issued a statement to the effect that, 'He is no more dangerous than any other murderer.'

THE LEAST SUCCESSFUL CHORAL CONTEST

A unique choral competition was held in Wales within the last two years. Only one choir entered the contest and even then it only managed to come second. The choir failed to win first prize, the judges said, as a punishment for arriving forty-five minutes late.

THE WORST FOX HUNT

There is a fox hunt somewhere in the North of England that has not killed a fox since 1901. Despite this crucial omission they dress up in traditional red hunting coats, drink sherry in large quantities and make all the right noises. They then ride over neighbouring fields in the full knowledge that all foxes have been systematically kept down by local farmers for almost a century.

I am told that between the wars they killed a hare. The hunt master is reported to have said: 'What happened? A horse step on it?'

THE LEAST SUCCESSFUL
AUDIENCE PARTICIPATION

The growing trend towards audience involvement has given us all the opportunity to add to theatrical confusion.

During 1974 a young woman attended a performance of the rock musical *Godspell* in London.

During the interval, the cast invited members of the audience up on the stage to meet them. She is said to have left her seat, walked down the arcade outside and passed through the stage door. After climbing a flight of dark stairs, she turned right and found herself on a brilliantly lit stage.

To the great surprise of herself and everyone else, she found herself in the middle of the cast acting *Pygmalion* at the theatre next door.

THE MOST UNSUCCESSFUL ATTEMPT
TO PROPOSE MARRIAGE

In the late 1900s a teacher in London was enamoured of a well-to-do young woman called Gwendolin who lived in Sussex. One weekend he went to the family's ancestral home near Lewes, to ask her to marry him. On his first night he woke at three a.m. wanting a glass of water. Feeling his way to the basin in the dark he knocked something over. Next morning he awoke to find that he had spilt ink over the priceless fourteenth century tapestry which was the pride and joy of Gwendolin's mother. He left immediately without seeing his beloved.

After the fuss had died down he returned to make another attempt. In order to minimize the chances of disaster he decided to call in for just half an hour in the afternoon. He asked Gwendolin's mother if he might speak to her daughter. While she was out of the room he sat down on what he took to be a cushion. It was however the family Pekinese, which did not survive the experience. He left again without seeing her. They both married other people.

THE BURGLAR WHO CALLED THE POLICE

A New York burglar committed what many admirers regard as the perfect crime in 1969. Following a carefully prepared plan, he climbed up on to the roof of a supermarket which he intended to burgle.

Once there, he discovered that he could not enter the building since the skylight was marginally too small to slip through.

With a sudden flash of inspiration he removed all his clothes and dropped them in through the skylight intending to follow them seconds later. Brilliantly, he was still unable to fit through and had to call the police to get his clothes back.

THE LEAST SUCCESSFUL HOUSEPARTY HOLIDAY

Attracted by the prospect of meeting 30 new people, a London solicitor booked a place on a houseparty holiday for young singles in Austria. When he arrived, he was the only person who had chosen the holiday.

THE WORST JUROR

There was a rape case at a Northern Crown Court in the late 1970s at which, according to a local crime reporter who covered the case, a juror fell fast asleep. Then the victim was asked to repeat what her attacker had said prior to the incident. Overcome with embarrassment, the girl was allowed to write it on paper.

This was then folded and passed along the jury. Each member in turn read and registered surprise on seeing words to the general effect that 'nothing in the whole history of sexual congress equals the comprehensive going-over which I intend *vis à vis* your good self'.

Sitting next to the dozing juror was an attractive blonde. After reading the note, she refolded it and nudged her neighbour who awoke with a start.

He read the note and looked at the blonde in wonderment. To the delight of the entire court, he then read it again, winked at her and put the note in his pocket.

When the judge asked him for the piece of paper, the recently dormant juror refused to hand it over, saying that it was 'a personal matter'.

ELEVEN

THE ART OF BEING WRONG

THE ART OF BEING WRONG

Being wrong is a natural gift. You cannot learn it. Some of us have a particular genius in this direction and can be wrong for months at a time.

The following is a selection of the statements proved most wrong by posterity.

'Heaven and earth were created all together in the same instant, on October 23rd, 4004 B.C. at nine o'clock in the morning' – Dr John Lightfoot, vice-chancellor of Cambridge University just before the publication of Darwin's *Origin of the Species*.

'Rail travel at high speed is not possible, because passengers, unable to breathe, would die of asphyxia' – Dr Dionysys Lardner (1793–1859), professor of natural philosophy and astronomy at University College, London. He also asserted that no large steamship would ever be able to cross the Atlantic, since it would require more coal than it could carry. Two years later the *Great Western* crossed the Atlantic.

'Animals, which move, have limbs and muscles. The earth does not have limbs and muscles; therefore it does not move.' – Scipio Chiaramonti.

'Far too noisy, my dear Mozart. Far too many notes.' – The Emperor Ferdinand after the first performance of *The Marriage of Figaro*.

'Stanley Matthews lacks the big match temperament. He will never hold down a regular first team place in top class soccer.' – Unsigned football writer when Matthews, the future captain of England, made his debut at the age of 17.

'If Beethoven's Seventh Symphony is not by some means abridged, it will soon fall into disuse' – Philip Hale, Boston music critic, 1837.

'I played over the music of that scoundrel Brahms. What a giftless bastard! It annoys me that this self-inflated mediocrity is hailed as a genius. Why, in comparison with him, Raff is a genius' – Tchaikovsky's diary, 9 October 1886.

'Flight by machines heavier than air is unpractical and insignificant, if not utterly impossible' – Simon Newcomb (1835–1909). The first flight by the Wright Brothers eighteen months afterwards did not affect his opinion.

'I can accept the theory of relativity as little as I can accept the existence of atoms and other such dogmas' – Ernst Mach (1838–1916), professor of physics at the University of Vienna.

'We don't like their sound. Groups of guitars are on the way out.' – Decca Recording Company when turning down the Beatles in 1962. (The group was also turned down by Pye, Columbia, and HMV).

'Rembrandt is not to be compared in the painting of character with our extraordinarily gifted English artist, Mr Rippingille' – John Hunt (1775–1848).

'The energy produced by the breaking down of the atom is a very poor kind of thing. Anyone who expects a source of power from the transformation of these atoms is talking moonshine' – Ernest Rutherford (1871–1937) after he had split the atom for the first time.

'They couldn't hit an elephant at this dist . . .' The last words of General John Sedgwick spoken while looking over the parapet at enemy lines during the Battle of Spotsylvania in 1864.

'You will never amount to very much' – A Munich Schoolmaster to Albert Einstein, aged 10.

'There are too many books. I shall never write one.' Stephen Pile – December 1977.

MEMBERSHIP
APPLICATION FORM
FOR NTGCGB

Name ....

Address ....

....

....

Exams failed ....

....

Main areas of incompetence (give details) ....

....

....

Subsidiary areas of incompetence: ....

....

....

Cases of sustained chaos occasioned by any of the above:

....

....

I would like to attend next year's International Festival of
incompetence at the Royal Albert Hall.

I am interesting in demonstrating my main area of
incompetence at the festival.

*Please place tick or cross in the box.

HEROIC FAILURES

THE OFFICIAL HANDBOOK OF THE NOT TERRIBLY GOOD CLUB

STEPHEN PILE

WITH TERRIBLY GOOD CARTOONS BY BILL TIDY

All Futura Books are available at your bookshop or newsagent, or can be ordered from the following address:
Futura Books, Cash Sales Department,
P.O. Box 11, Falmouth, Cornwall.

Please send cheque or postal order (no currency), and allow 30p for postage and packing for the first book plus 15p for the second book and 12p for each additional book ordered up to a maximum charge of £1.29 in U.K.

Customers in Eire and B.F.P.O. please allow 30p for the first book, 15p for the second book plus 12p per copy for the next 7 books, thereafter 6p per book.

Overseas customers please allow 50p for postage and packing for the first book and 10p per copy for each additional book.